Advance Praise

"This book has changed my financial and personal life. I love the practical, easy-to-follow seven-step system. After following The Financial Freedom System for over a year, I have witnessed my relationship with money positively evolve and shift. I now feel more peace, calm, and stability in my finances, where I often felt stressed and lacking direction. But the great news is that this book offers so much more than a system of building financial freedom and good money habits; it's actually a transformative guide for personal change and empowerment. That's why I highly recommend this book to anyone seeking financial freedom and a life of greater choice. Read The Financial Freedom System. It will change the way you think, feel, and act with money forever."

—JENNIFER MARR, author coach and book specialist

"The power of money and the financial system is real. You can let that power control you, or you can follow Daniel's system and take your power back."

—DAN O'SHAUGHNESSY, Founder of OSF Partners

"I highly recommend this book to anyone interested in saving more money by using the power of your intuition while eliminating stress. It will show you how to build wealth through positive energy. Every parent needs to share this with their kids!"

—KATHY WICKMAN, retired mom

"For me, this is such a simple system. Daniel has a special relationship with God and his own intuition; it's truly a remarkable gift. My favorite part is that it's not about the money. I thoroughly enjoy learning from Daniel. Having peace of mind and developing my intuition has been invaluable to me. Thank you, my friend!"

—TONY TIEDEMANN, Founder and CEO of Tiedemann Globe

"I have been working with Daniel since 2012. I have been fortunate enough to follow the Financial Freedom System. It works! I have been able to be calmer and more confident with my financial foundation, which has freed me up to make significant changes in my life and thrive. The system is simple and requires dedication but is worth it. I can't recommend it enough."

—MATT CURRY, CEO of Giant Results

"People's relationship with money is like a baby to dynamite: ignorant and dangerous. Daniel's new book defuses your money dangers by providing a 'conscious' path for creating happiness and purposeful wealth in your life."

—CHARLIE EPSTEIN, financial advisor, actor, entertainer, and entrepreneur

"Daniel's Financial Freedom System is an easy-to-read guide to gaining and growing your financial success. Following the seven principles in this book will accelerate you toward achieving your financial goals and give you the confidence of being in total control of your money."

—BOB CACCIABEVE, CEO of EZ RED

"*Daniel is a gift to us all! He is at the cutting edge of understanding how to use the forces of the universe to create incredible abundance in every aspect of your life. I have known and worked with him for many years, and I can truly say that his mentorship and teachings have resulted in outstanding mental, spiritual, and financial gains for me and my family.*"

—MARK LACHANCE, CEO of Maxy Media
and bestselling author of *The Lucky Formula*.

"*I always had a fear of never enough. So much insecurity. Through Daniel's teachings, I have practiced exactly as is written until they became habitual. Now the words 'gratitude' and 'abundance' are part of my everyday life. At last I can breathe. Thank you, Daniel.*"

—STEPHEN THOMPSON, Founder of Breathing Soul

"Our relationship with money and finance can have a tremendous impact on our sense of general well-being, happiness, and success in life. Daniel White's Financial Freedom System *is a practical yet philosophical way for anybody to reset how they think about their personal finances. Then they can become free to pursue the many gifts that life presents when one is not weighed down by the stress of money."*

—FRANK LAMAR, DDS, clinician, educator, and serial entrepreneur

"When I first started working with the Financial Freedom System, *I had no savings even though I owned a multimillion-dollar business. The system shifted my mindset to one of abundance versus fear. I had no idea the burden living paycheck to paycheck was having on me until I was free from it. I was held captive by the idea of not having enough instead of understanding that money is just a tool to be leveraged. This book is a must-read for everyone."*

—LISA M CINI, President and CEO of Mosaic Design Studio

"If you want financial freedom, inner peace, and greater stability in your life, read this book. Why? Because the Financial Freedom System taught in this book works!"

—DR. BENJAMIN HARDY, organizational psychologist and author of *Be Your Future Self Now*

"When Daniel White tells me to do something, I've learned to do it. You'd be wise to follow my lead, read the book, and do what he says. You'll be happy you did."

—TUCKER MAX, four-time *New York Times* bestseller

"Having worked with Daniel for the last twelve years, I can confidently say he has greatly impacted every aspect of my life. This book is the most unique I've ever read on money. Daniel takes you to the root of what creates wealth and then provides a complete system to create financial freedom."

—GINO WICKMAN, author of *Traction and The EOS Life*

"Having known and worked with Daniel for over seventeen years, I can tell you that The Financial Freedom System comes from a unique perspective and is grounded in deep experience and practice. There are a lot of books about intuition and a lot of books about money—this is the first one that marries the two together with practical results proven over twenty years."

—BABS SMITH, Co-Founder and CEO of Strategic Coach

"Move over, Dave Ramsey! Daniel masterfully gets to the root cause of money insecurity at all income and asset levels and gives a clear roadmap to achieve financial freedom while saying no to stress, ego, and external pressures. This book is a must-read for those looking to manifest more money freedom by gaining awareness and security about your finances!"

—BEN LAWS, CEO of Evexia Wealth

"What an awesome book! This thoughtful and practical system will transform your relationship with money from one driven by ego, fear, and scarcity to one driven by confidence, love, and abundance. Invaluable!"

—SHANNON WALLER, author of *The Team Success Handbook* and *Multiplication by Subtraction*

THE
FINANCIAL
Freedom
SYSTEM

THE
FINANCIAL
Freedom
SYSTEM

An Uncommon Guide to Master
Your Money and Transform Your Life

DANIEL WHITE

THE FINANCIAL FREEDOM SYSTEM
An Uncommon Guide to Master Your Money and Transform Your Life

FIRST EDITION

ISBN   978-1-5445-3998-0 *Hardcover*
       978-1-5445-3996-6 *Paperback*
       978-1-5445-3997-3 *Ebook*
       978-1-5445-3999-7 *Audiobook*

Contents

Why I Wrote This Book and How You Will Benefit from Reading It

I PROMISE THAT IN THE YEARS TO COME, AS YOU EXPE-RIence a life of freedom, growth, stability, and abundance, your future self will thank you for choosing to take on my Financial Freedom System.

Many books teach how to become wealthy or retire rich by following a path based on other people, economic factors, electronic systems, or structures in the external environment. However, I have not seen any that focus solely on addressing the core issue of your unconscious programming nor use your intuition as the guiding force for your transformation, as my system does. The truth is this system has the potential to positively benefit all aspects of your life. My frustration with the fact that no one was teaching this information drove me to share my story and my system. I believe in self-empowerment and have set out to create a book that gives the power back to you.

The seven-step system I have developed provides an easy-to-follow, stress-reducing long-term road to peace of mind, stability, and freedom. It transforms your dependence on others so you can stand in your own power.

Because of the results I have experienced in my life and witnessed in the lives of my clients, I am sharing this system with you. When you experience stress around money and finances, it is challenging to connect with your intuition and find the strength to develop your God-given gifts. The system described in this book will free you to pursue inspired direction and purpose for the rest of your life.

Before you begin, it's important to understand that if you love the addiction to financial stress and the negative effects it has in destroying peace and abundance in your life, this book is not for you!

Contents

On the other hand, if you wish to experience true freedom with regard to your finances and are open to transforming your life, read on, because this book is dedicated to you.

To your freedom,

Daniel

A System to Become Financially Free and Wealthy for Life

I REMEMBER VERY CLEARLY THE DAYS WHEN I FELT constant stress about money. I worried about how I was going to generate income, find my next clients, or get ahead financially. I spent many sleepless nights worrying about my bills and how I would pay them. During these times, I experienced a total lack of self-confidence and became exhausted to the point of numbness, and yet I was still unable to sleep.

At the same time, I felt ungrounded, as if I were adrift in my life with no foundation. As a result, my actions lacked strength, power, and certainty, so I was unable to manifest my dreams and goals. It was like a waking torture, and I longed to remove it from my life.

Realizing I could not continue like this, I decided to change my financial beliefs and habits forever in order to create a life I would love. This single decision not only shifted my financial situation, but it also profoundly changed the course of my life. Intuitively, I knew there had to be another way to manage money. So, I began developing a system that could help everyone avoid the emotional pain and suffering financial stress produces.

After years of experimenting with my own money, I created a Financial Freedom System that works for me—one that gives me ongoing peace and ease in handling my finances. As I worked with clients, I found many were struggling financially and emotionally due to their lifestyle choices. Sometimes they were barely surviving, let alone breaking even with their money. So, I decided to share with them the secret of how I freed myself from this debilitating and soul-destroying lifestyle.

After successfully teaching my clients this system, I could see that anyone can create a life of ease and peace of mind around money by following the steps I've devised. At this point, I knew it was time to share all I have learned with as many people as possible. I am doing that here within the pages of this book.

The good news is the system is easy to use and simple to understand. I have also kept this book—and the explanation of the seven steps—*short* and *to the point* so you can quickly and easily implement the steps on your journey to creating financial freedom.

To be clear from the outset, this isn't a *get-rich-quick* book. Instead, it is a *become-wealthy-for-life* book, which shows you an effortless yet transformative long-term system that will provide many years of abundance, peace, and freedom—gifts that money alone can never buy. The power of my system manifests through transforming *you* to the very core of who you are, because you choose your consciousness around your life, your home, your family, and yourself.

KEY PRINCIPLES

The transformational impact of this system is based on the following principles.

Reconnecting with God

Your 100 percent commitment will give you strength and close any gaps where fear or doubt can sneak in and sabotage your goal.

Trusting Your Intuition

When you follow your intuition, life flows for you. When you pray or speak with God, your intuition is God answering you.

Protecting Your Environment

When you protect your home and environment from negative influences, you remain clear and grounded.

Leading Yourself into Action

You become the master of your life as a whole by first mastering your ego, habits, unconscious patterns, and, of course, money.

This system will help you find the inner guidance that fills your life with joy and ease. Once you follow this financial system consistently, all other areas of your life will miraculously improve, including health, family, relationships, career, and happiness. This is a wonderful side effect of committing to this transformational journey.

To achieve financial peace of mind and gain these additional benefits, you need to reprogram your unconscious financial habits to break free of struggle-and-survival mode. Once this is achieved, you can step into the consciousness of abundance and relaxation around money. You will create new energy and fresh habits that offer inner security and stability. This, in turn, allows life to flow for you and not against you.

HOW THIS SYSTEM WORKS

The system is based on seven simple steps I developed over the course of three decades through trial-and-error experimentation. Along the way, I had many successes and just as many hard lessons. Sometimes I thought I was progressing, but then my ego would interfere, sabotaging all my efforts and taking me backward, away from my search for financial peace and abundance. When I use the term ego, I refer to the lower self, fears, negative human tendencies, perceived weaknesses, and habitual thought processes that block perception of natural intuition and connection with God. Learning how to be more aware of your ego and its influence is an essential part of the transformation process.

The key to the success of the seven steps is that they accomplish the following:

- Help you to **stop digging** yourself further into a financial hole.

- Guide you to **shift your focus toward freedom** and raise you out of your financial hole.

- Provide simple, practical processes to **begin building** a financial foundation.

- Support you in your choice to **become conscious** about how money flows through your life.

- Start an inner transformation so you can **reach financial stability** with ease and peace of mind.

- Assist you to **stand on solid financial ground**.

- Empower you to **achieve financial freedom** and move forward in life.

Furthermore, while helping clients all over the world apply my system, I have seen it work for everyone who has implemented and completed the seven steps over time. It works, as long as you are **committed to following all the steps**, because the system is designed to create a transformation at the unconscious level of your mind. This inner transformation will bring peace and abundance into your life.

Now after many years of practicing and refining these steps, I have no stress about where my future income will come from or when my next client will turn up, as life flows with ease, abundance, and joy. As a result, my life has now changed from being a struggle to becoming a fun adventure. It is that simple, and if I can turn my financial life around, so can you. You have nothing to lose and everything to gain by committing to the seven steps.

As you progress through the seven steps of The Financial Freedom System, I recommend that you write about your thoughts, feelings, challenges, and wins in a notebook or journal. Or you can purchase the specially designed Financial Freedom Journal—details are at the back of this book. By journaling about your experiences, you will gain greater strength and profound insights related to your beliefs and habits around money. This will help you let go of those that do not support you and build on those that do as you steadily grow your foundation.

How Thirty-Five Dollars Transformed My Life

THROUGHOUT MY LIFE, I HAVE BEEN SURROUNDED BY people who are either savers or spenders. I know some people who save every penny they can, live within their financial means, and spend only the minimum amount on living expenses. They look for the best deals when buying items and ensure there is always money in their bank accounts. Instead of using credit, they pay cash for everything they purchase so they don't incur any debt or unnecessary expenses. Interestingly, I encounter these people across all financial levels, from those on small incomes to extremely wealthy individuals. These are the savers.

I know other people who spend money freely without thinking about how much they spend or where their money goes.

They buy the latest high-tech toys or cars, eat in expensive restaurants, go on many holidays, and usually use credit to pay for it all. So, they not only spend what they have, they also incur debt. I also find these people across all income levels. These are the spenders.

I can see that the spenders tend to live day by day, pursuing short-term pleasure without a clear financial plan for the future. Even though they often earn a good income and appear to be materially successful, underneath they are usually stressed about money because they don't take the time to create a solid financial foundation.

On the other hand, the savers respect their money and strive to create wealth and security over the long term. They spend less than they earn and save over a lifetime. They also have a plan for their financial future and understand that progressing toward goals takes time, which results in a sense of peace, stability, and freedom around money.

Which Path Would I Follow?

For years, I was unconsciously pulled in different directions with my finances. I saved, then spent, and then saved again. When I found the self-discipline to save up and finally break even, I invariably spent my savings on some toy or experience that threw me back into financial struggle. It was a stressful and unsustainable way of handling my finances, and I wanted to end this roller-coaster ride.

At the end of April 1999, I celebrated my fifth year in business and realized I had nothing to show for all my hard work. Not only did I have no savings or assets, I also had large credit card debts from five years of using these to pay for marketing and promotion for my growing business.

I was totally dejected with my financial situation. No amount of wishful thinking would save me. No miracle was coming. I knew that if I wanted to see a change in my financial situation, I had to change my actions.

MY BIG BREAKTHROUGH

I made a decision. I decided to change my financial situation. There was just one problem: I had no idea how to do it. I spent the next month trying to think of ways to transform my business. Most of them were crazy money-making schemes, and none were viable. All required an investment of more money, which I didn't have.

Then, my intuition chimed in and reminded me of the times I had flown in airplanes as I traveled around the world. It whispered to me, **"Remember the airline safety drill. Put on your own oxygen mask first."**

Suddenly, I got the message and knew exactly what to do. I realized I'd been doing the opposite with my money by paying everyone else first—the landlord, utility companies, and other business expenses. By handling my money in this way, nothing was left to pay me. I had been starving myself and my business of financial oxygen!

At the beginning of June 1999, I decided to pay myself first before anyone else. I promised myself that every Monday morning I would go to the bank and put thirty-five dollars into a savings account, which I called my Foundation Account.

However, when the first Monday arrived, I didn't have the full thirty-five dollars in my wallet to make my deposit. I rummaged through my house and car until I found enough coins to make up the difference. I didn't want to take the easy way out and go to an automatic teller machine (ATM) at the bank to withdraw the money. I wanted to challenge myself, and I had faith this plan would work.

So, I swallowed my pride and walked down to the bank with my bag of coins and dollar bills to open my account. My hands shook as I filled out the paperwork for my new account and then gave the bank teller my bag of money to be counted and deposited.

The teller gave me a deposit book that showed my account details with my thirty-five-dollar balance on the first line. I was about to learn that when you make a strong decision and follow through with action, opportunities flow toward you.

As I walked out of the bank, I saw on the pavement right in front of me a fresh twenty-dollar bill. Surprised, I bent down and picked it up and looked around to see if anyone nearby may have dropped it as they passed the bank. However, the street was empty. As I held the money in my hands, a sense of calm confirmation flowed through me. It seemed that by taking this very small step of opening my Foundation Account and depositing my money, I had already begun to move toward the abundance I sought. It was an amazing feeling.

From that day onward, every Monday morning, I walked to the bank and deposited my thirty-five dollars. Over the weeks, the total amount of money in my account grew, and so did my confidence.

Sure, this wasn't going to get me out of debt, allow me to buy property, or let me retire, but I had a rewarding feeling of satisfaction in knowing I was growing my Foundation Account. As my business grew, I slowly increased the weekly deposit from thirty-five dollars to fifty dollars to eighty dollars and eventually to one hundred dollars.

After a few months of making my weekly deposits, I had a huge breakthrough of awareness with my Foundation Account. **I realized I wasn't trying to get rich. Instead, I was in search of a mind free from stress and a body full of peace.**

I explored different ways I could use money to reduce stress and create peace. I found the first answer in experimenting with the amount of cash I carried. If I had two hundred dollars or more in my wallet, I felt peaceful and relaxed. On the other hand, if I had less than that, I felt stressed. So, I made a decision to always keep a minimum of two hundred dollars in my wallet.

After a couple years of making weekly deposits into my Foundation Account, the balance increased to more than five thousand dollars. At this point, I felt a new level of peace within my body. Suddenly, it didn't matter how much money

I had in my wallet. I still felt the same level of peace and freedom.

I call this five thousand dollars my Critical Mass. In high school, I had learned that Critical Mass was the amount of uranium-235 needed to start a nuclear reaction. In scientific terms, it's the point where abundant energy is created. Once I had achieved this financial Critical Mass in my Foundation Account, my unconscious mind let go of a tremendous amount of stress, further relaxing my body.

Of course, the two-hundred-dollar and five-thousand-dollar amounts were the levels at which I personally felt peace, stability, and freedom. You'll discover your own financial comfort levels as you progress through the seven-step system.

Step 1:
Decide and Commit

ALL GROWTH STARTS WITH TAKING ACTION BELOW THE neck. If you want something to change in your life, simply thinking about it, talking about it, or visualizing it won't change anything. You also have to take inspired action.

When you visualize or talk about making a change, the energy lasts only as long as you keep thinking about it. Then, just like switching off a computer screen, it is gone. Therefore, it is only a mental exercise.

Remember that below the neck is the part of your body that takes physical action. This part of the body moves you forward and is vital for change to occur. I often say to clients, "How far would you go in life if you had only a head with no body?" Likewise, if you become stuck in your head thinking about things but not taking action, you get caught above your neck, making it difficult to move forward.

In that case, your life would be stuck in all thought and no action. However, when you act on your thoughts, you move toward what you want in life. This is the power of taking action below the neck, because it makes the desired change a reality.

Deciding is making a choice above the neck; committing is taking action below the neck. The word *decide* comes from the Latin term *decidere*, which means "to cut off." When you make a strong decision and commit to a particular path, you cut off alternative choices available to you. Therefore, to make a decision and commit to it is a potent step to moving forward.

Power is created when deciding on a course of action and then committing to follow through with your decision. Deciding can also assist you in overriding environmental influences.

When you make a strong decision to start The Financial Freedom System and experience its transformational process, you start to attract God's light to you. This light builds your energy to move toward freedom. By making this one decision and then taking action, you will experience a subtle increase in your energy and resolve, which will have a ripple effect across all areas of your life.

On the other hand, when you have not made a decision toward positive change, you attract energetic darkness, fear, and egocentricity, which slow you down. Over time, the darkness might paralyze you more and more. Remember, even strongly choosing not to decide is a decision that is empowering.

The question is *do you want a peaceful life, or do you want to continue to experience stress?*

Be courageous and make use of the energy, power, and sense of purpose you feel in this moment, or old habits will soon exert themselves and sabotage your efforts to change. Make your decision and commit to taking action on the journey of transforming your life while your energy levels are high. To strengthen your decision to act on building your financial foundation, use your journal to reflect on the reasons you want to commit to financial freedom.

YOUR FOUNDATION: YOUR ESSENTIAL BASE FOR LIFE

There's a reason I use the word foundation to describe the account you will use in the transformational process to create peace of mind and freedom in your finances: **we all need a solid foundation or base to be able to stand up for ourselves and move forward with courage, creativity, and freedom**. For a child to achieve the early milestones of standing and then walking, the infant has to push against a solid surface, such as the floors in the family home, the earth under its feet, or other firm, climbable objects, to engage its muscles and propel its body upward and forward.

However, if children just dreamed of, thought about, or visualized themselves standing and walking, this mental activity would remain unrealized and stuck in their minds. Because of this, the energy would not reach their leg muscles to engage them into action to stand or walk. Without action, this energy remains trapped in the body and creates a buildup of emotion, which then turns into frustration and stress because the energy has nowhere to go.

The creation of a strong foundation is key to success, so it is essential that you build your foundation for yourself.

THE BUTTERFLY'S STRUGGLE

I remember hearing a story about the transformation of a caterpillar into a butterfly that beautifully demonstrates the need for having a foundation. The story goes something like this:

> A boy found a cocoon in his garden and saw the butterfly inside was trying to break its way out to freedom. However, as he watched the butterfly struggling to leave its cocoon, he could see that the hole through which it was trying to escape seemed too small for the creature. Feeling concerned, the boy thought it would be a kind gesture to help the butterfly break out of its cage by making the hole in the cocoon larger. So, he ran inside and grabbed a pair of nail scissors and carefully cut down the side of the cocoon so the butterfly could easily wriggle its way out to freedom.
>
> Once the butterfly was free, the boy felt satisfied with his assistance to this beautiful creature. He then waited to see the butterfly open its wings and fly away. However, he noticed its body was shrunken and withered, while its wings were small and shriveled. So, the poor creature could only crawl around on its legs and could not fly.

The boy was devastated to learn that, as part of the butterfly's final development, it needed to struggle to break free of its cocoon. In fact, the act of pushing itself through the small hole was essential to strengthen the butterfly and build its wings. In doing so, the butterfly would only then be fully formed and able to fly.[1]

Like the butterfly, you will go through a transformational process as you build your foundation.

It is time to decide and commit for yourself today. This important first step will give you an immediate surge of personal energy and inner commitment to propel you toward financial freedom. Take this step now, and you will feel a subtle, lasting shift in your beliefs and self-worth.

YOUR PERSONAL COMMITMENT TO FINANCIAL FREEDOM

Begin your financial freedom journey today and commit to the process by answering these simple questions:

---

1 Adapted from the story by Sonaira D'Avila on the Lesson of the Butterfly, as mentioned by Paulo Coelho, https://paulocoelhoblog.com/2007/12/10/the-lesson-of-the-butterfly/.

- When will you commence The Financial Freedom System—today, tomorrow, this week, or this month? Enter your start date here:

_____

_____

_____

- What is your greatest reason for committing to The Financial Freedom System? This will support your 100 percent rock-solid commitment. Please write your reason for commitment:

_____

_____

_____

- What is your current annual income?

    * Before taxes:

_____

    * After taxes:

_____

Becoming Conscious of Your Money

If you don't know your annual income (before and after taxes), it's important to calculate them now before you move on so you're conscious of your money situation. Being unconscious about your income is like not wearing your oxygen mask in a plane when it's losing air pressure—it will suck the money right out of your life.

How to Calculate Your Current Annual Income

If you are already established in your career, ask your accountant, or look at your last year's tax return. For those who are just starting out in a career, working part time as students, enjoying casual employment, or collecting government assistance, add up your income for the past month and multiply it by twelve months to gain an approximate annual income figure.

Why You Need to Know Your Annual Income Before and After Taxes

Many people spend money based on their income before taxes. Then they get angry with the government when they have no money left each month because they resent having to pay their taxes. So, they blame the government (and anyone other than themselves) for their financial situation. Personal responsibility is lacking with this attitude.

It's empowering to know how much money you earn in gross annual income, how much you receive as net annual income, and how much goes to the government in taxes. It is a key part of the process because it helps you become conscious about the actual amount of money you have available to spend.

It is critical to your success to first know what is real for you now before you begin your journey to building your foundation. Similarly, if you want to use a map to travel across an unfamiliar city, the first thing you need is your starting location. Your current reality is the starting point to planning your financial future.

STEP 1 CHECKLIST: DECIDE AND COMMIT

- **Decide** to transform your life into a new experience of freedom, peace, and abundance. To strengthen your decision, recognize that you are also choosing to overcome perceived weaknesses in the area of finances and money management. Every day, say out loud with conviction, "I choose to create financial freedom in my life." Write this on a sticky note and place it where you will see it daily.

- **Commit** to taking action below the neck, beginning on the date you chose in the section titled "Your Personal Commitment to Financial Freedom." Then decide which day of the week you're going to make your deposits. I recommend Monday mornings to train your unconscious to pay yourself first every week.

- **Take action** by writing down your answers to the questions in the "Your Personal Commitment to Financial Freedom" section.

- **Record** details about your transformational journey to build your foundation, including thoughts, feelings, and insights. Use a notebook or journal, or buy the companion Financial Freedom Journal (details are in the back of this book).

COMMON QUESTIONS ANSWERED

How will I know I'm ready to commit to building my foundation?

Any time is a good time to start, but if you are sick and tired of being stressed about your financial situation, today is the best time to decide and commit to building your foundation. As the old adage says, "The best time to plant an oak tree was twenty years ago; the second best time is now."

By taking this first step, you can turn your anger and frustration with your current financial circumstances into life-changing action. Your future self will be thankful you did, so consider starting today.

What can I do if I feel hesitant about taking this first step?

Any hesitation is your ego trying to block your growth. This will occur if you are not fully committed to building your foundation. In this case, doubt and fear will find a gap in your commitment, and your ego will assert itself in an attempt to stop you from transforming your life.

31

Ask yourself if you truly want financial freedom, and if so, decide and commit 100 percent to taking action toward building your foundation. This is your first step toward transformation.

If I am married or in a committed relationship, should I set up a shared Foundation Account with my partner, or is it best to build separate foundations?

I recommend that each person in a partnership has their own separate Foundation Account to gain the transformational benefits. As each of you builds your own foundation, you raise your own energy. Then, together as a couple, your combined energy magnifies to raise your creative power in a partnership and as a team. Everyone benefits in ways you could never imagine.

I have seen many couples experience greater cohesion and more happiness as they progress through the seven steps to build their own foundation. This can be achieved even if one partner or spouse stays at home to care for children or does not earn money outside of the home. In this case, the at-home partner builds their foundation from their discretionary funds or housekeeping budget.

Is it okay to tell others I am building my financial foundation?

I answer this question in four ways, with one "No" and three "Yeses":

No, not initially, especially if you have chosen to follow The Financial Freedom System on your own.

As part of your commitment to yourself and your financial freedom, resist the temptation to tell everyone you meet about your Foundation Account goals. Instead, remain silent about your new plans because telling others about your goals before you build strength in your actions or reach your Critical Mass might dissipate your energy, particularly if others question or place doubt on your efforts. This energy is the vital impetus you need to keep moving forward with your financial transformation.

This is a good lesson for all areas of your life because talking diffuses energy, so you defeat yourself when you talk about taking action instead of actually doing it. This is why it is best to not tell others about your plans when you start your journey to build your foundation.

Yes, if you are following The Financial Freedom System with a dedicated group or are joining our events.

Some people have greater success by being part of a group of like-minded people when moving forward with their goals. This is especially true if you feel you lack the strength or commitment to do it alone, and it helps with accountability. Therefore, creating or joining a group can be powerful as you'll gain support and inspiration by interacting with aligned, aware individuals who are also on the financial freedom journey.

If this is the case for you, I recommend creating or joining a dedicated Financial Freedom Mastermind Group and committing to following the full system together. Ensure that the individuals you invite to join are as committed to their success as you are to yours. You can choose to meet weekly, monthly, or quarterly to encourage one another, offer support, and act as accountability buddies as you complete the steps. Together you can share insights and celebrate your successes.

I also conduct regular events to answer your questions and invite you to join these practical, informative, and empowering online get-togethers. Details for these events are also found in the back of this book.

Yes, as you progress through The Financial Freedom System and experience breakthroughs.

As you begin your transformational journey with money, positive experiences and synchronicities will be reflected in your life as evidence of your progress. This is why recording your transformations in your journal is so important. During this time, you will feel more grounded and confident, and you can then share your experiences with others.

Some people will likely notice your shift in stability and peace, questioning what changes you have made. Share The Financial Freedom System with them if your intuition guides you to do so.

Yes, once you have reached and passed your Critical Mass.

Once you have reached and passed your Critical Mass in Step 6, you will have built great strength in your foundation. After completing that step, share this book with anyone you feel you can support in the growth of their Foundation Account.

If you have any specific questions on Step 1 and would like them answered, write them down here or in your Financial Freedom Journal and join our next online event. See details in the back of this book.

Step 2:
Envision a Full Tank

Having a clear vision of the transformation you'll experience by building your foundation is very important. This gives you the all-important initial energy to take the first physical action toward achieving your goal. Therefore, it is essential to see your financial tank as full.

THE WARNING LIGHT IN YOUR BODY

Having your Critical Mass in the bank is like driving your car with plenty of fuel in the tank, while having less than your Critical Mass in the bank is like driving at night with the low-fuel warning light flashing, not knowing where you will find the next fuel station. You'll always feel more relaxed driving when that warning light is off and your tank is full. Likewise, reaching your Critical Mass allows you to move forward with a greater sense of confidence and certainty in life.

Interestingly, once I achieved my Critical Mass, I attracted new positive opportunities and more prosperity in my business and personal life.

Unfortunately, when my Foundation Account grew past this level, my ego kicked in and said, "I want to make this go faster!" As a result, I took money out of my Foundation Account to invest in some stocks and business ideas. In doing so, I also bought myself a major learning experience. I noticed that whenever my Foundation Account dropped below my Critical Mass amount, my investments always failed and stress returned to my body.

So, I had to go back and rebuild my Foundation Account. Once I built it back above my Critical Mass and kept it there, my body relaxed again and my investments succeeded.

How Will It Feel When Your Tank Is Always Full?

If you follow the simple yet profoundly effective steps I outline in this book, you'll be able to look back in five or ten years and be thankful for these benefits:

- Your financial life runs like a car that always has a full tank of fuel.

- You have extra money available to you at the end of every month.

- You feel an overall sense of peace you couldn't have imagined experiencing before you implemented this system into your life.

- Your intuition grows clearer and stronger over time, and you have the energy to take action on your gut instincts.

- You have 100 percent of your annual income sitting in the bank, and you don't need to touch it.

- You've developed great relationships and new friends who are living abundant, energetic lives.

THE FINANCIAL FREEDOM SYSTEM

- You have access to your God-given talents and the freedom to share them with other people.

Imagine how that will feel! This is what it means to live with an abundance mentality.

Abundance Mentality

Someone who has an abundance mentality doesn't worry about missing the boat on an opportunity because they believe there is plenty for everyone and that opportunities are always available. They know God is always looking after them, so they have a mindset of faith. I have many clients who are highly successful and demonstrate an abundance mentality. They have the following qualities:

- They have a strong personal foundation.

- They approach life decisions in a realistic manner and take time to make wise choices, as they know there is no need to rush important decisions.

- They have an extremely good gut instinct, which they follow because they are not stuck in their heads, in hype and ego or the influence of others.

- They are uncomplicated, genuine people who often prefer the simple things in life.

- They live life according to principles, not ego, and always build for solid growth.

- They surround themselves and collaborate with people who possess the skills that complement the needs of their family and business.

- They grow their finances like a solid oak tree, not like a seasonal perennial.

I also find that abundance-minded individuals choose to handle the following financial elements in ways that may surprise you.

Taxes

They take care of their taxes. If you don't file your taxes and pay immediately when they are due, you connect with the collective stress of others with unpaid taxes. I am sure you have felt the overwhelming burden of having to get your taxes done. This can be true even if you are expecting a tax refund and especially if you are expecting a tax bill.

If you want to go to the next level of abundance, file your taxes on the first possible day of the new financial year. I experimented over the course of a few years with how energy affects us at the time we file and pay our taxes. If I get my taxes done quickly, I feel the release of a burden I didn't know existed. As a result, I now enjoy feeling more relaxed in my body. When my tax bill comes in, I pay it immediately, as I put money away every month into my tax savings account to pay it in full.

As I teach this to my clients, they are amazed at the increase in their energy levels.

Bills

People with a mindset of abundance pay their bills before they are due. I recommend paying your bills as soon as they arrive, not by the due date. This sets up the consciousness that you always have money and that you honor the suppliers and providers from which you have already received goods and services. After all, you don't pay for a restaurant meal thirty days after you have eaten it, do you? No, you pay for it straight after you have eaten your meal and always before you leave the restaurant.

In 2001, I decided to pay the rent on my home and office three months in advance. What I noticed was astounding. Suddenly, the landlords and their managing agents treated me very differently than how I had been dealt with in the past. As a tenant, when I called the property managers regarding an issue with the building, I received immediate attention. Anytime I asked for assistance, nothing was too much trouble. I was treated with respect, courtesy, and goodwill because I always paid the rent in advance.

When it was time for me to move to a new home in 2002, the landlords did not want me to go. They actually said, "No, you can't leave us. Is there anything we can do to make you stay?"

It was fascinating, and I came to see the power and benefit of keeping my bills paid in advance and in good stead with my creditors. I saw how I could apply this lesson in other areas of my life and money management.

Credit Card Debt

Abundance-minded people understand debt and are happy to pay off their debts while building their foundation. They use their credit cards wisely and always pay off the balance each month. To them, a credit card is a financial tool to record expenses, not an instrument for buying instant gratification.

When I finally paid off all my credit card debt in 2007, I made the commitment not to take on anymore debt for a few years. Instead, I decided to turn my credit cards into credit-holding instruments so I wouldn't pay interest on any purchases. As I still wanted to use the credit cards as an expense-recording tool, I deposited up to $2,000 on each card, above the zero balance, so I always had funds available on the card when I purchased something. When I used the card, the product or service was automatically paid for by the credit balance. To maintain my positive credit balance, I deposited extra money onto the card after I used it so I always had interest-free funds available on my credit cards.

Mortgage

Those with an abundance mindset don't buy a home to keep up with appearances or for reasons of status. When you buy a new home, always purchase within your current reality and financial means. Then improve the existing property or move to a better one as your means and abilities increase. By taking the longer-term approach, you base your decisions on the foundation of truth and reality, not fantasy. Following this course of action means you will be able to increase your wealth over your lifetime. Remember, there is no rush over the long term.

Car

They purchase their car within their financial means and pay cash for it, rather than using leases, installment plans, or loans. Those with an abundance mentality manage their financial responsibilities and debt in ways that may seem quite opposite to how financial institutions and societal expectations often encourage us to deal with money and credit.

Having an abundance mentality is the opposite of feeling stressed and fearful about money. So, always be mindful of who you take your financial advice from.

Stress Is Not Your Best Friend

One client was building her Foundation Account and growing her business at the same time. She came to see me in a stressed state because she was getting advice from a so-called successful businessman. He told her she should invest money in buying a great deal of stock as well as supplies for her business for the future. Her intuition told her not to take his advice, and as a result she felt confused. I simply asked her, "Does this man have a solid foundation?" Immediately she realized he didn't. He was extremely unstable in his life, and she understood her intuition was trying to warn and guide her away from making a poor choice.

Your awareness of your intuition increases as you build your foundation, and stress levels decrease in your mind and body. This allows you greater energy to take action that follows your intuition. Visualize your new reality to begin creating your financial freedom. As you complete this step, you will see opportunities to make an even greater commitment to your financial future.

STEP 2 CHECKLIST: ENVISION A FULL TANK

- **Acknowledge** how much you have in your bank account right now.

- **Check in**. How do you feel about your current balance? Write it down here.

_____

_____

_____

- **Visualize** having the equivalent of 100 percent of your annual income, before taxes, in your bank account.

- **Check in again**. How do you feel about your projected balance? Write it down here.

_____

_____

_____

- **Compare** the two feelings. Which feeling do you prefer and why?

For most people, the image of having a full tank makes them feel more relaxed and less burdened with stress.

When I created this exercise, I found myself struggling to breathe during my first visualization. When I visualized the second image, my body began breathing on its own. I thought, ***Why not make this vision and this feeling the reality in my life and my bank account?*** And that is exactly what I did.

COMMON QUESTIONS ANSWERED

What if I experience fear or stress during this process?

If you are taking your first couple of steps below the neck, be aware that if something threatens or frightens you, your habitual reaction might be to shift your focus back to over-thinking above the neck. This fight, flight, or freeze reaction will keep you stuck and stop you from moving forward with your commitments, because fear pushes your focus away from being grounded in your truth.

This transformational system teaches you to flow through life instead of living in fear. Follow each step of the system, becoming aware of any fear that arises, and continue to persevere to neutralize the fearful energy. Over time, your fear will lessen and disappear as peace, strength, and stability increase.

What does "being conscious" about my money mean?

Being conscious about your money means having the power to know how money flows in and out of your life, and also how other people influence your flow of money. The gift of this is that it is easier for you to make decisions aligned with your intuition when you are financially conscious because this gives you power over money instead of money having power over you.

People who are in financial stress and struggle typically don't have budgets or order in their money management, or they have no money management at all. Therefore, they have little control or consciousness of their money flow. Budgeting is a way of knowing how to distribute your funds, and this provides you clarity and intention with your finances.

At one time I was trying to live a champagne lifestyle on a beer budget, living beyond my means. It disrupted my financial position and caused great stress in my life. Many years ago I wanted to visit the Bahamas for a holiday and was particularly excited about going, as I had never been to these islands. Yet, as I planned my trip and considered where I would stay, I realized I had no clarity and found the process challenging. It didn't feel right for some reason, and I wondered why, because I really wanted this dream holiday.

I soon understood my feelings were mixed because I didn't have a budget for my holiday. As a result, I had no idea how much I could spend on accommodations, entertainment, sightseeing, dining, and other daily expenses. This lack of clarity around my money meant I had no idea how much I could comfortably spend, so I experienced discomfort every time I tried to plan the details.

I realized if I had a budget, I'd know exactly where to stay, how much to spend, and when I should travel. It was an important lesson, as being conscious of your money situation gives you power and control in your life.

Can I skip the early steps and just start making deposits?

No. It is important that you follow all seven steps in the system and complete them in the correct order. Think back to your experiences of learning at school. Just imagine what would happen if you were studying a new area of mathematics and then missed a few days of school right in the middle of lessons about the key concepts. This would undoubtedly cause a gap in your knowledge, so when you returned to class, you would not understand the lessons that followed because you had not learned the preceding concepts.

The same is true for building your financial foundation. You cannot shortcut the process, and all seven steps must be followed as part of the below-the-neck transformation process.

If you have any specific questions on Step 2 and would like them answered, write them down here or in your Financial Freedom Journal and join our next online event. See details in the back of this book.

Step 3:
Calculate Reality

Your next step is to calculate the amount neces-
sary to start building your Foundation Account. This
amount needs to be real for you and not inflated by your ego
or others' influences.

Choose an amount for your weekly deposit that fits into
your current budget and doesn't cause you financial stress.
Your correct deposit amount is one you won't miss in your
present financial situation.

Make calculations based on where you are now, **not** where
you'd like to be or how financially successful you may have
been in the past.

LET GO OF YOUR EGO

When calculating the amount of your initial deposit, be aware of your ego's attempt to influence you. Your ego will tell you a small deposit is a sign you are cheating in some way or not taking the system seriously. On the other hand, starting with a deposit that is too high is also your ego attempting to influence your decision, to create more stress for you.

To establish just the right deposit amount to begin with, keep lowering your dollar amount to avoid being triggered by your ego. Once you feel a sense of inner peace, you've reached a point that indicates your correct starting amount.

Be careful not to compare your deposit amount to your annual income. This can be a real deal breaker right at the beginning of your journey, potentially leading to depression and frustration, as well as sowing the seeds for future self-sabotage.

SIZE DOESN'T MATTER

It's not the size of your deposit that matters—it is the consistent action and growth that transforms you and your life.

I want to show you an example of growth to give your mind and ego some ease with the slow pace of The Financial Freedom System.

Remember, this is only an example. Your unique process will come by trusting and following your intuition.

If you deposit just one dollar in the first month—roughly twenty-five cents per week—and then double your deposit each month (my recommended maximum increase amount in Step 5), this is what will happen to your monthly deposits within eighteen months:

- 1st month: $1

- 2nd month: $2

- 3rd month: $4

- 4th month: $8

- 5th month: $16

- 6th month: $32

- 7th month: $64

- 8th month: $128

- 9th month: $256

- 10th month: $512

- 11th month: $1,024

- 12th month: $2,048

- 13th month: $4,096

- 14th month: $8,192

- 15th month: $16,384

- 16th month: $32,768

- 17th month: $65,536

- 18th month: $131,072

Wow, after only eighteen months, your monthly deposit is above most people's annual income! However, let's not get ahead of ourselves.

You can see that after six months of following the process, your deposits are only $32 for the month, or roughly $8 per week. This is typically not a great deal of money compared to an annual income, but after twelve months, your monthly deposit is over $2,000, and your total accumulation is $4,095.

The point of this is to demonstrate that if you start with a deposit amount which is in integrity with your current reality, your Foundation Account will grow over time. This is the power of growing your deposit regularly, which is addressed further in Step 5.

As you take the time now to focus on and calculate your financial reality, you reinforce and expand your capacity to take action and move steadily toward financial freedom.

A client explained this realization when she took the time to calculate her financial reality. *She felt as if a light bulb had gone off in her mind and saw her finances differently. She experienced a sense of integrity and responsibility around her money and couldn't wait to start building her Foundation Account.*

THE POWER OF RECORDING YOUR RESULTS

One client explained that she not only records and reviews her progress in her journal, but she also uses a whiteboard in her home office to track her foundation deposits. To set up this visual tracking system, she first wrote this affirmation in the center of her board: "I choose to create financial freedom in my life." She then listed each month of the year down the side of the whiteboard, and as she calculated her weekly deposit amount for each month, she recorded the dollar figure next to the corresponding month. After she made her weekly deposit at the bank, she placed a checkmark next to the weekly amount until she had completed all of her deposits for the month. At this point, she recorded her end-of-month Foundation Account's total balance next to the collection of checkmarks.

Every time she sits down to work, she sees her Foundation Account slowly and steadily growing over time. Additionally, she also sees her deposit amount increasing and can appreciate how far she has progressed. Her whiteboard serves as a constant reminder of her commitment to herself, her family, and her financial future, and helps keep her steadily on track.

I'd love to hear about your experiences as you progress with building your foundation. Please find details in the back of this book on how to contact the team and share your story with us.

STEP 3 CHECKLIST: CALCULATE REALITY

- **Ask God** to strengthen your intuition so you can gain the best results for your deposit amount. Partnering with God also helps you overcome your ego.

- **Calculate mentally** (above the neck). Work out your whole financial situation and budget. Then think of a deposit amount you will be able to handle and not miss each week.

If the amount creates stress and tension in your body, then it's too high. You can start with any amount—fifty cents, one dollar, ten dollars, or twenty dollars. It doesn't matter. What's important is that you feel at ease with your amount. As you deposit the money and your unconscious energy shifts, the amount you can comfortably deposit will grow.

Before you can get there, you must establish integrity with your present reality. I even had a wealthy client who started with just twenty-five cents per week.

- **Calculate emotionally** (below the neck). See yourself depositing this amount each week. Does your body feel relaxed? If not, lower the amount until you feel at ease. Don't build your financial foundation with your ego, or it will fall apart like a house of cards when the strong winds of life blow your way. Also, do not, under any circumstances, compare the amount of your deposit with your annual income, as this will create stress.

COMMON QUESTIONS ANSWERED

How will I know when I have found my correct deposit amount?

Calculate mentally and then calculate emotionally to arrive at your deposit amount. You will feel completely relaxed in your body and mind when you deposit the correct amount, and if you have any hesitation, reevaluate. It is better to deposit less and feel comfortable than to deposit more and invite your ego in to take you off course.

Do I have to start with small initial deposits?

It depends on your current financial consciousness. You may have already established an unconscious foundation earlier in your life. As a result of this, your initial deposit might be larger. However, if you haven't already established an unconscious foundation, your initial deposit might be very small.

Either way, your deposit amount totally depends on your current circumstances, and it is essential that you do not compare the size of your deposit amount with other people's. This is particularly true when partners or couples are establishing their own Foundation Accounts. Do not compare your deposit amount to your partner's, as this is your transformational journey and no one else's.

If I am already wealthy due to my family's financial status or an inheritance, does this affect my deposit amount?

If you have inherited wealth, you may not have developed any unconscious, personal financial foundation at all and thus you will have a small initial deposit. I have found this situation common with the third generations (and even later) of a family's inherited wealth. However, do not let a small deposit amount concern you, because overcoming your ego and trusting your intuition will be a major blessing for you as your life transforms.

If you have any specific questions on Step 3 and would like them answered, write them down here or in your Financial Freedom Journal and join our next online event. See details in the back of this book.

Step 4:
Deposit at the Bank

IT'S NOW TIME TO BEGIN BUILDING YOUR FOUNDATION BY making your first deposit.

At this stage, perhaps you feel nervous or a little uncomfortable. You could be unconsciously scared to relax because you may be accustomed to the adrenaline, cortisol, and norepinephrine hormones your body produces when in a constant state of stress. The thought of financial freedom may initially be appealing, but then your stress addiction kicks in and stops you from taking action to create a new reality.

So, the question becomes "What state of mind and body do you choose?"

If you choose peace, nurture the crucial new habit of paying yourself first. Taking action below the neck in Step 4 brings inner contentment and peace of mind as you build greater financial security. This, in turn, enables you to move toward a better, more creative, productive, and fulfilling life.

Soon, the habit will become natural, easy, and enjoyable.

OPENING YOUR FOUNDATION ACCOUNT AT THE BANK

Once you have determined your correct deposit amount, it is time to take action and open your Foundation Account at the bank:

- Visit your bank in person and ask a teller or other associate to set up your Foundation Account. Select a bank that is easy for you to visit on a weekly basis.

- Request key features, such as a deposit-only bank account, with low or no fees, and with interest applied to your balance.

- Ensure that you can make your cash deposits at the bank, or if you have to make your deposits after banking hours, via an ATM.

- Commit to making weekly cash deposits in person and on the same day each week.

- Make sure your deposits are in cash, not by check, and under no circumstances make your deposits via a set-and-forget electronic transfer from one account to another.

Remember, your weekly deposits must be made in cash and in person. Each time you make a deposit, you'll experience an increased level of energy and peace. At first, you might find the energy shifts are subtle, depending on how deeply embedded your old habits have become. However, stay with your commitment to the process and continue to make your weekly deposits, as most of my clients experience an increasing uplift within the first thirty to sixty days. Over time, greater energy and peace will come as your unconscious is transformed. Much like when you plant a seed in the ground, it may take a few weeks before you see visible signs of growth.

Some of my clients tell me they felt embarrassed and unworthy to go into the bank and make their deposit because the initial amount was so small. When a client tells me they are embarrassed to make small deposits, it shows me how much power they are giving to their ego or other people's opinions. Unfortunately, these influences can dominate their lives, causing them to spend beyond their means. This type of thinking builds up stress in the body, so these clients suffer due to their attempts to keep up with others or follow an unrealistic ideal, rather than honoring their own reality.

It often comes down to the financial examples and spending dynamics set by family during their foundational childhood years. If their family educated them wisely about money, this could have provided them with an early financial foundation model to follow. Yet, if they received no financial education or had poor role models, they must now learn how to build and maintain a financial foundation for themselves.

Interestingly, other clients share that they experience a deep sense of joy and happiness as they make their deposits each week. This shows they are aligned with their transformational goal, so their spirits celebrate as they take this new action in life.

One client says she feels a sense of joy and fulfillment as she drives down to make her deposit at the bank each Monday morning. It's even become a task she looks forward to each week. She explains that it's as if a calm knowing has risen up from within to now gently guide her every step of the way. She no longer feels fear, stress, or confusion around her finances—an unhealthy dynamic that had been her reality for many years. Instead she has found a steadily growing sense of peace and order, which expands with every deposit she makes into her Foundation Account. For her, it has become more about how she feels and less about her account balance.

BREAKING THROUGH THE EGO

Another client underwent a personal breakthrough when she pushed through her ego's resistance to correctly set up her Foundation Account and follow the guidelines of my system.

Years ago, this client attended my seminar on "Building a Financial Foundation," prior to publication of my first book, *Is Your Money Running on Empty?* However, instead of making her foundation deposits in person and in cash, she decided to take a shortcut. Disregarding my advice, she chose to set up an online savings account with weekly electronic transfers into her Foundation Account. By doing this, she didn't have to go into the bank each week. As she made regular money transfers and saw her savings account balance growing, she thought she was on track to building her foundation.

However, as long as she used this process, she found that something unexpected always happened to require her to spend some of these funds. Therefore, she was unable to build and maintain a strong foundation because she did not gain the transformational effect of making her deposits in cash and in person. This kept her in a state of frustration and stress in her financial life, until one day she finally understood the concept!

Years later, after reading the first edition of my book, she took action below the neck by driving straight to the bank to set up a Foundation Account. Yet, it seemed life wanted to ensure she was fully committed this time around, because setting up her Foundation Account was not a straightforward experience.

First, she chose to establish her Foundation Account with a small local bank with which she had not previously had any dealings. When she went to set up the account and make her first deposit, the bank teller told her she had to make an appointment with an account manager and return the following week. As she booked her appointment, the teller assured my client it would be a quick process to establish the new account and she needed to bring only her driver's license as proof of identity.

The next week my client returned to the bank and met with the account manager. They had almost completed the setup of her new account, but unfortunately, my client's driver's license had recently been renewed electronically but she hadn't yet received her new ID card, which had been sent via the postal service. Her expired license was invalid as proof of identity. She couldn't set up her Foundation Account on that day unless she had further identification, such as a passport. The account manager suggested she come back at another time to complete the account setup.

However, my client was 100 percent committed to opening her Foundation Account **that day** and nothing was going to stop her. By this stage in her transformation, she had completed the first three steps of her journey:

1. Decide and Commit

2. Envision a Full Tank

3. Calculate Reality

And she was determined to take action on the fourth:

4. Deposit

She drove home for her passport and went back to the bank so she could make her first deposit. In the end, she had to visit the bank three times, but she had finally learned to push through her ego's resistance in order to follow through with her commitment to change her financial situation.

As my client shared her story with me, she explained that as soon as she made her first deposit into her Foundation Account, she felt a calm sense of purpose around her finances. Immediately she felt more positive and confident as her intuition guided her actions. That week she picked up two new clients in her business and unexpectedly received a small refund check from her old bank. These small events were signs that she was on the right path to building her foundation. Most importantly, she knew nothing could stop her from following her transformational goal, and she couldn't wait for the following Monday to come around so she could make her next deposit.

This can happen for you also. When you look back in six to twelve months' time, and then again in a few years, you'll see how much you have grown. You'll feel a great sense of achievement and satisfaction as you take charge of your financial life. I recommend that each month you celebrate how much your foundation has grown since you started making your deposits. This celebration will also expose any ego or arrogance that may try to sabotage your progress.

It's a great idea to use your Financial Freedom Journal to record the positive thoughts and feelings you have as you make your deposits and watch your Foundation Account grow. You can also write down any ego, arrogance, and negative chatter that gets exposed while following this system. Additionally, you can reach out to me or one of my team members for a one-on-one session or join in on one of my Group Transformation Sessions to clear and transform any blockages. See the back of the book for details.

GROWTH TIPS

The following ideas will assist you in prioritizing the action of paying yourself first and maintaining your Foundation Account deposits before you make purchases.

A great habit to get into before you buy anything at the store or online is to ask yourself, "Have I paid myself first this week?" Do this exercise before every buying activity, and you'll quickly develop the habit of giving to yourself first before mindlessly giving your power, energy, and money away to others. If you ask yourself this question and the answer is no, stop the transaction and first put this week's deposit into your Foundation Account. Be vigilant with this exercise to prevent your ego from sabotaging your transformation.

One client was out shopping for a new electronic device and realized he hadn't made his Foundation Account deposit for the week. He quickly remembered the importance of asking himself, "Have I paid myself first this week?" When he answered no, he took action. He immediately left the store and went straight to his bank to make his weekly Foundation Account deposit. Afterward, he returned to the store to complete the transaction. However, when he went to pay for the item, he found he no longer had any desire to purchase it.

This change in how he felt about the device showed him his ego had been influencing him to spend money unnecessarily.

Another habit to develop is asking yourself the following question before springing for a second cup of coffee or buying that shirt you don't need just because it's on sale at a bargain price: "How would I feel with 100 percent of my annual income sitting in the bank right now?" When I ask myself this question, I usually feel a sense of inner peace and realize I don't need to make the purchase after all.

This question will reawaken the feeling you had when you first visualized having 100 percent of your annual income in the bank in Step 2. Reconnect with that perspective, and you'll dissolve all the fear and stress that would have caused you to haphazardly give away your power, energy, and money. It will help you regain your power to make purchases when you need them, not because other people or energies influence your thinking and spending.

OPTIONAL STEP 4: THE JAR PRINCIPLE

Over the course of teaching my Financial Freedom System, I sometimes work with clients who initially do not want to make their deposits into a bank. For some, this is because they are embarrassed by the size of their weekly deposit amount, and others simply don't trust banks.

The latter was a very real issue during the global financial crisis of 2008. To address these concerns, I experimented with different ways of containing and growing money to build a foundation without going to the bank. From this I created another highly effective system I call **The Jar Principle**. It is easy to implement, and it is just as powerful in its transformational effect.

Using a Jar to Build Your Foundation

The Jar Principle is based on the concept of putting away or containing money, just as you do with a bank account, except you do this process at home. When I first experimented with this idea, I used an old spaghetti sauce jar. I simply washed it out, cleaned the lid, and made deposits into the jar as I would with my Foundation Account at the bank. The jar became my new foundation bank account in December 2008. You can use a box instead of a jar, as long as you can securely close the lid. Some of my clients use a shoebox, which they've decorated.

Each time I made a deposit into my jar, I placed the cash inside and then screwed the lid back on. I came to understand that once I place the cash inside the jar, it is very important to reseal the lid. This not only contains the money securely, but it also reinforces within my unconscious the action of protecting money. In contrast, if I leave the jar open without the lid firmly in place, I feel there is no strength in my action and the energy of the money is not contained. I've learned that the jar has to be closed to hold the energy and create the transformational effect.

When my jar was so full that I couldn't reseal it, I changed many coins into notes, and then eventually changed the notes into gold and silver coins or ingots. I did this to transmute the value of my Foundation Account savings into hard, usable currency, and I stored these in a safe. That way, if cash was devalued in the future due to inflation, I could still buy the things I needed by trading these precious metals, as they would likely retain or even increase in value and purchasing power.

Follow the Same Steps

If you choose to use The Jar Principle, it is exactly the same as going to the bank, except you make your deposits into your sealed jar. As with your bank Foundation Account, record your start date and initial deposit amount, and then each week, deposit money into your jar.

One client who uses The Jar Principle purchased a velvet drawstring bag to sit inside her jar. Each time she makes a deposit into her jar, she first puts her weekly money into the velvet bag and then returns the bag to the jar. She explains that she loves feeling the weight of the bag growing each time she makes her deposit of coins and notes. The velvet bag also increases the containment of the money and its energy. Other clients store their sealed jars inside a home safe to create a similar effect. Some clients use The Jar Principle at home for their weekly deposits and then go to the bank monthly or every other month to deposit the accumulated money into their Foundation Accounts.

Don't Drain the Jar

If you take money out of your jar to deposit it into a Foundation Account or into a safety deposit box at the bank, **you must leave some of the money behind in the jar** as seed money for your next weekly deposit. This maintains the energy consciousness in your jar to keep you moving forward. From my experience with clients, if you remove all the money, the energy you have built up will dissipate and you might easily forget to make your weekly deposits. This is especially important if you haven't yet reached your Critical Mass amount.

STEP 4 CHECKLIST: DEPOSIT AT THE BANK

- **Open** your Foundation Account at the bank. Find an account that doesn't attract high fees, at a location where you can make your deposits in person or through the ATM as opposed to online.

- **Make your deposits** in person. You must make your Foundation Account deposit with your own hands. Having someone else do it for you won't work, and neither will making the deposit by electronic transfer. Only you can transform your unconscious and develop your new financial habits. That is why you must physically take your deposits to the bank.

- **Check in** with your feelings. As you make each deposit, notice how you react to the situation and be aware of the thoughts that arise. This will reveal any weaknesses in your foundation. Write about your insights in your Financial Freedom Journal.

- **Celebrate** each month to honor how much your foundation has grown since you started making your deposits as a way of acknowledging your progress.

COMMON QUESTIONS ANSWERED

Why do I have to make my deposits in person and in cash?

This is the question asked most often, and my answer is always the same, "You must take tangible, consistent action below the neck." At this point in the system, it may seem difficult to understand the importance of making deposits in person. However, if you don't make your deposits in cash and in person, you will not build a strong foundation and transform your unconscious behaviors.

Once you consistently follow through on your commitment to make your payments in cash and in person, you will experience the satisfaction of taking solid, concrete action. You will feel responsible, honest, and authentic around your money situation. This will help you overcome your ego's pull so you can build your foundation.

Why don't electronic transfers support my progress?

I have experimented with making deposits by electronic bank transfers and found it doesn't have the same transformational effect on my unconscious mind. Doing the deposit process via electronic transfer is great for a traditional savings account strategy. However, it does not work as a lifetime transformation strategy for building a strong foundation.

What if I go on holiday and can't get to my bank for a few weeks?

If you're planning to be out of town for a few weeks, place your weekly deposits in your Foundation Account in advance of your trip. This way your unconscious can relax while you're on holiday.

Do I need to pay off my debts before
I start my foundation?

No. It's important to know you can still build your foundation while you are reducing your debt. Therefore, do not let your debts stop you from beginning your Foundation Account. Just as your body is always replacing old cells with new ones, you can put new thoughts, practices, and habits into your mind, body, and life without first having to get rid of the old ones.

In my experience, when I focused only on paying off my debt, I was caught in the energy of debt so there was no financial growth. I was energetically connected to my creditors, and this kept me financially stuck. I needed to focus on the balance between building up my own energy while slowly letting go of the energy of lack or debt. You will expand your strength and courage over time, and your debt becomes easier to eliminate as you shift your energy to that of abundance.

While I was building my Foundation Account, I slowly reduced my debt. During this time, I wondered how I would feel once I was debt-free and imagined how much less stressed I would be without debt in my life. As my financial strength and foundation grew, I was finally able to pay off all my debts. It felt amazing to reach this point.

My next goal was to have no outstanding debt for two years and to experience what it felt like to be debt-free for a period of time. I ended up remaining this way for four years before I took on any new debt. It was a liberating and transformational experience. I also found that my foundation strength grew larger the longer I was without debt.

For The Jar Principle, can I use a money box in place of a jar?

No, you cannot use a traditional money box. These typically have an open slot in the top or side where you make deposits. They don't ever fully seal, so the financial energy you build with each deposit escapes through the open slot. The box or container you select for your Jar Principle deposits must be resealable.

If you have any specific questions on Step 4 and would like them answered, write them down here or in your Financial Freedom Journal and join our next online event. See details at the back of this book.

FREEDOM BREAKTHROUGH: INTEGRITY

Congratulations!

Once you have done Step 1 through Step 4 and made your initial deposit, you've reached a breakthrough point in the transformation of your relationship with money and finances. Be truly sincere with this stage of the process, as it will strengthen your results for your future. The key is to be in a state of **integrity** with your deposit calculation.

This means you are in **integrity** with your financial reality and not being influenced by your ego. Accept this is your current deposit amount based upon your present reality and deal with this truth. By doing so, you destroy the illusion of where you are financially, get real, and start to live more below the neck.

Step 5:
Grow and Protect

EVERY WEEK, MAKE REGULAR DEPOSITS TO GROW YOUR Foundation Account. Then, every month, increase the amount of your weekly deposits, even if only by a little, and always only to a level that's comfortable within your present reality. The size of the increase is totally up to you and how you feel when you consider your new deposit figure. No one will judge you for the amount of your increase, and it should not be determined by ego-based drives. Some months you may not feel the need to increase the deposit amount at all, and other times, your deposit increase may be significant.

It's fine to be ambitious, but don't increase your deposit to more than double the amount of the previous month, even if you think you can handle the increase. This can invite your ego to play tricks on you, and you need to avoid this at all costs. Instead, maintain a deposit increase that is in alignment with your present circumstances and energy. After a few months, you'll notice subtle changes in your consciousness.

Each month as you recalculate your deposit amount, you are training yourself to listen to and follow your intuition. This will help improve your ability to trust your intuition in other areas of your life and lessen your ego's influence, providing you with many profound benefits.

It will take time to see the cumulative results of your initial deposits, and these little increases are essential in this process. It is important that each deposit increase feels solid and gives you a renewed sense of excitement, energy, and enthusiasm for the transformational system you are following. As you progress, you'll look forward to the next month's increase and notice a sense of positivity running through your body.

This is a sure sign you're shifting to a state of being in charge of your money instead of letting an ego-based perspective of money be in charge of you.

GROWING IN STRENGTH WHILE YOU REST

As an athlete, I learned that my strength did not increase on my hard exertion training days. It happened on my easy recovery days and during my sleep. If an athlete continually pushes through training without any recovery time, the constant physical stress might feed their ego but will eventually result in breakdown or injury.

The same goes with your Foundation Account. If you are always pushing to grow the size of your account by increasing deposits more than once a month or to a point where you feel uncomfortable or by doubling your last month's deposit, you feed your ego and lose connection with your authentic truth. When this happens, you may make mistakes with your finances or even lose everything.

Accordingly, some clients have found that their deposit amount does not always increase between months, even as they are building their financial strength during this period. They do not feel comfortable with an increase, so they maintain the same deposit level for a month or two, and this is fine.

Do not be disappointed if you feel the need to stay at the same deposit amount as your previous month. It simply means you need more energy stored in your system before moving to the next level. Think of how children often gain "puppy" fat before they grow in height—this is stored energy for the next growth spurt. Your body (below the neck) may need more time to integrate the new changes into your unconscious. When this happens, focus more intently with your deposits during the next month to embody this new level of your foundation. If you are patient with this situation, it will later pay off for you massively.

DEPOSIT INCREASE TIP

Those who start with a relatively large weekly deposit amount may find monthly deposit increases are smaller in size. This may astound you, but it is perfectly acceptable. The key is to make only a deposit increase that is in line with where you are in the present and to continue depositing regularly.

The lesson here is to **be stronger than your excuses**, because if you get bored with the project, you'll stagnate and go back to your old habit of struggling with your finances. Stay strong and focused on your commitment to your transformed future.

BREATHING IN, BREATHING OUT

One great way to stay on track with your Foundation Account goal is to do the following breathing exercise. Through my exploration on how to quiet the mind and reduce levels of fear and anxiety in the body, I came across a study from neuroscientist Jill Bolte Taylor, PhD,[2] author of *My Stroke of Insight*. In her book, she explains our ability to change our blood chemistry in ninety seconds or less. Basically, it takes less than ninety seconds for an emotional program to surge through the body and then be completely flushed out of the bloodstream. Through self-sabotaging thoughts, we choose to continue feeding the emotion, in turn keeping the corresponding hormones or internal chemicals surging through our physical system.

I was so happy to find this science-backed information, as I had been teaching a similar concept for many years. During my running career back in the 1980s, I found that if I did deep breathing for two minutes before the start of a race, my pre-race stress and anxiety disappeared. In fact, sometimes I was so relaxed that I momentarily fell asleep and had to be woken up because the race was about to start! During the

---

2   Bolte Taylor, PhD, Jill, "Own Your Power," in *My Stroke of Insight* (London: Penguin Books, 2009).

times I was totally relaxed prior to my race, I achieved my best performances. Deep breathing was that effective.

I teach this two-minute breathing process to my Financial Freedom System students to practice each time they make their deposits at the bank or in their Foundation Account jars. This helps them overcome any embarrassment, greed, insecurity, and other ego-based influences that might sabotage them from transforming their financial habits. The more they practice the exercise, the stronger they and their Foundation Accounts become. Of course, you can do this breathing exercise for more than two minutes. Some clients choose to start the breathing process when they arrive at the bank and continue until they leave—except, of course, when they are talking with the bank teller.

The exercise is done by breathing in through the nose for around four to five seconds and out through the mouth for six to seven seconds, in a continuous cycle for two minutes. This is roughly ten breath cycles. I have found the shift in energy occurs around the point of seven or eight breaths, which corresponds with Dr. Taylor's findings regarding the transformation in ninety seconds or less. I recommend that more advanced clients complete one minute of breathing in through the nose and out of the mouth, and the second minute breathing only in and out of the nose. Some clients do the whole two minutes breathing in and out through their nose only.

AIM FORWARD, MEASURE BACK

Another great lesson I learned during my career as a runner was to have goals to aim for and then to measure back to see how I was improving. When I tried to focus only on the goals ahead of me, I was frustrated with my progress, which often led to training issues and injuries. However, when I appreciated how much I improved each week or month, I felt a freedom in my body and enjoyment in my sport.

I remember during one running program in late 1994, I started an intensive training session and was ready to quit after completing only 15 percent of the workout. As lactic acid built up in my body and exhaustion set in, I focused on how much more I had to do to complete the training session and how hard it would be to finish the other 85 percent of the workout. With this type of thinking, I was soon ready to quit.

I then shifted my thinking to focus on each small part of the workout and how much I had already achieved. I looked ahead to the future, and instead of perceiving difficulty, I checked my feelings on how I would feel after completing the training session versus quitting. It was clear I felt so much better imagining myself completing the goal. Before I knew it, I was 90 percent of the way through my training session. This was an enormous breakthrough in my ability to change my perception of how to work through and complete a task when I was tired. I soon applied this lesson in many areas of my life, including my finances.

FOCUS ON THE BABY STEPS

From my running experience, I realize that when I focus only on the end goal, I expend too much energy on an ideal that is beyond my present capabilities. In turn, this leads to feelings of disappointment and frustration that push me toward giving up on the process and letting the ego win.

Place your focus on each weekly deposit and on the feeling you get when you visualize your end goal—100 percent equivalence to your annual income in your Foundation Account. Give all your attention to today's task so you can build the foundation layers to the next level on your way to the end goal. If at any time you experience frustration, focus more intently on the baby steps of this week's growth action, and add enthusiasm to the action when you have any small wins.

When you aim for the feeling of a stress-free relationship with money and measure back to how much you're growing, you protect yourself from sabotaging your future goals. If you become frustrated by your slow progress in the first few months of using this system, remember to breathe and turn this energy of frustration into the energy of determination!

This is only a test to see if you're serious about transforming your life. Measure back to where you were at the start of your journey and realize that if you had not started this process, you wouldn't have any of the money you've collected in your Foundation Account. See this as a significant improvement in your life, and don't let your frustrations take you backward. Instead, let challenges inspire growth toward your goals. You can also read back through your journal to review the subtle transformations you have already achieved.

THE FIRST NINETY DAYS

One of my clients was just over ninety days into her journey with the system, yet she had already experienced a number of profound benefits in her life. She explained that as she began her fourth month of making deposits and building her Foundation Account, she experienced a feeling of greater appreciation, gratitude, and generosity. Plus, when her habitually stressful thoughts about finances arose, she was able to recognize them and let them go. So, she felt more stable and in the flow as her life progressed with more ease and calm.

She also gained greater clarity with her business and planned to release new products and services, as well as complete her end-of-financial-year tax requirements before they were due. In the past, getting her taxes completed on time was always a struggle, and she was often late with submitting them. Her accountant was very happy with this change! In addition, new clients began to flow toward her, all without effort on her behalf. This was the shift she had been looking for, and she found it as she followed each step of the system.

SHRINKING THE GAP BETWEEN IMAGINATION AND REALITY

One client shared with me how he experienced a major shift in the way he felt as he built his Foundation Account over time. In Step 2, when he first visualized his money in the bank, he experienced feelings of lack, insecurity, and scarcity. He felt uncomfortable with this as his reality. Then, when he visualized having 100 percent of his annual income in his Foundation Account at the bank, he experienced feelings of peace, freedom, prosperity, and stability. He felt grounded and solid. So, there was a large gap between how he felt with his current financial circumstances and how he imagined he would feel once he reached his goal. To him, it seemed these two contrasting financial realities were miles apart.

Even so, he continued to make his weekly deposits into his Foundation Account. Over time, as his Foundation Account grew, he noticed the feeling he experienced in his present reality was slowly getting closer to the feeling he had when he visualized having his 100 percent annual income in the bank. This was because the initially large gap between his reality and his goal was shrinking as he took action below the neck to bring his current reality toward his visualized future. Each week the emotional gap became smaller, and inwardly he felt better. Correspondingly, this subtle inner shift in his energy began to be reflected in his outer world in terms of happiness, stability, and opportunities.

Fortunately, he had been recording his journey in his journal and was able to recognize these changes in his life and celebrate his wins each step of the way.

PURCHASING TIPS

Do all you can to protect yourself from ego-based drives and influences. Overcome your fears by developing new habits around making purchases. First, when you're about to buy something, notice how you feel. Are you strong and grounded, or weak and excited? Do you feel relaxed or stressed? Acknowledge your feelings, whether you're buying food, clothes, gifts, electronics, a new car, or even a new home.

Next, once you're familiar with the various ways you feel as you make purchases, build a new habit of buying only what strengthens you and not buying what weakens you. I do this every time I buy myself new clothes. I hold the clothes I want to buy and see how my body reacts to the fabric and color. If it is a shirt, hat, or glasses, I hold them close to my face and see how my body responds. If my body breathes on its own, I consider buying the items. For pants, jeans, shorts, or shoes, I hold them below my waist and see how my body responds. I listen to my body rather than what my eyes see or what the salesperson says.

One time while clothes shopping, my body rejected an item, but I was unsure why. I later found out the parent company of the brand was going through financial difficulties, so I could feel this energy in the clothes. Clothes are like a piece of art that contains the energy of the artist, whether that energy is positive or negative.

When you make purchases during this time, especially large ones, such as a car or home, spend within your current level of integrity.

STEP 5 CHECKLIST: GROW AND PROTECT

- **Reflect** each month on how much you can **grow** your weekly deposit without feeling stress. Make sure the amount is not more than double the previous month's deposit, regardless of how strong you feel. Do the breathing exercise before you calculate the deposit increase to keep ego from influencing your decision.

- **Protect** yourself by being mindful of your ego's attempts to stop, slow down, or sabotage the process. Ignore the thought that says, "This method doesn't work." Don't overspend because your ego says, "I really need and deserve this new toy!" This is blatant self-sabotage. Use your Financial Freedom Journal to measure the progress you have achieved since you started the system and write about any ego interferences along your journey.

- **Breathe** your way to financial freedom. Every time you make a deposit into your Foundation Account or jar, do the two-minute breathing process before, during, and after making your deposit.

- **Record** your results and notice weekly habits in other areas of your life. Put these notes into your Financial Freedom Journal.

- **Check in** with your feelings. Each month, repeat the visualization of your current bank balance and imagine your annual income in your Foundation

Account. Record in your journal any changes in how you feel about your current bank account balance.

COMMON QUESTIONS ANSWERED

Why are the deposit amount increases made only once a month?

When builders construct a multistory concrete building, it takes up to twenty-eight days for the concrete to cure enough to be able to handle the weight of the next layer of the construction. Using this building analogy, it is your job to take personal responsibility for getting yourself strong enough for the next stage of growth along your journey. I find it takes a month of weekly deposits at the new deposit amount to transition from the following:

- **First week**: A new level of deposit is established, which is a stretch from the previous month's deposit.

- **Second and third weeks**: Feeling comfortable with the new deposit level through building your inner strength creates a sense of grace and ease.

- **Fourth week**: You are ready to take the next deposit increase by building energy for your next growth spurt.

Will my deposit increase always be the same incremental size?

No. It will vary every month, depending on how your energy is utilized throughout the previous month and what your intuition perceives is coming in the next month. This is an intuitive transformational journey, and that is why you need to go within to feel what deposit increase level is right for you each month.

To test this, I once experimented with a separate Foundation Account, using a process of increasing the weekly deposit by exactly the same amount of five dollars every month. It was a very mental, above-the-neck system. Initially, it was easy, but then I felt like I was getting lazy with the process. I wasn't putting any of my below-the-neck energy into the process. Eventually, it turned into a traditional savings account as there was absolutely no energy of a transforma-tional nature in the account.

Another time, years after I had finished building my financial foundation, I experimented with the system again. I took myself through all seven steps, with my initial weekly deposit being $500, and the next month, it increased by only $10 to $510 per week. I was initially surprised with the small increase in the deposit amount, but I trusted in the system. The following month, my weekly deposit amount increased by only $4 to $514, which I found extremely surprising. However, it felt right for me and in keeping with my integrity. The next month, my deposit amount increased by $6 to $520 per week, and then the fourth month my weekly deposit amount took a big jump to $650— an increase of $130. So, you can see how the increases can vary month to month.

What if I realize I have increased my deposit by too much?

Stop and reevaluate the integrity of your increase for this month. Then continue by making deposits at the correct amount. This will give you greater peace of mind and ease with your money. Write in your journal about your experience of how your ego interfered with your intuition.

Another option comes from a client who felt extremely uncomfortable and stressed after she raised her deposit amount by too much. Suddenly, when she made her weekly deposit, she felt financially stretched, insecure, and fearful around her finances, instead of experiencing greater peace of mind. To correct this issue, she kept her deposit at the same amount for the following month so she could grow into a new deposit amount. After two months, she was able to increase her deposit amount again without stress. However, this time during her calculation, she followed her intuition instead of her ego, and she completed the breathing exercise to make sure the increase was aligned with her financial integrity.

Can I make additional deposits to my foundation over and above my weekly deposits?

No. Remember to keep your ego in check! Making additional deposits can sabotage your transformational journey because your ego will push you to strive for a financial result, rather than use your intuition to build a grounded and solid foundation. If you want to do something with your extra money, place it into a separate savings account or start the Managing Extra Money process in Step 6.

What if I stop making deposits for a long period of time? How do I start again?

If for any reason you stop making your deposits or are unable to do so for any period of time, don't lose heart or give up! Instead, recommit to The Financial Freedom System. Follow each step in order as you previously did and begin making your weekly deposits. As soon as you do this, you will feel a sense of calm and peace return to your body and mind. This is your intuition confirming that you are back on the right path. Continue to build your existing Foundation Account with the goal to reach your Critical Mass and beyond to your initial annual income level.

What if I go out of town and my time away crosses over into the next month?

Place your deposit in your Foundation Account in advance of your trip for each week you are away, so your unconscious mind can relax while you're gone. If your time away crosses into the next month, maintain the same amount of weekly deposit into this new month. You cannot guess what the new increase is going to be without first having the new levels of strength already built inside your unconscious. To speculate is to invite your ego to play games with you. Keep this same deposit amount going when you get back home until the start of the following month; then recalculate the new month's deposit amount.

If you have any specific questions on Step 5 and would like them answered, write them down here or in your Financial Freedom Journal and join our next online event. See details in the back of this book.

FREEDOM BREAKTHROUGH: INTUITION

Congratulations on reaching your next breakthrough!

Once you have calculated the increase amount of your weekly deposit, you have completed the next stage for the transformation of your relationship with money and finances.

Be sincere with this stage in the process as it will strengthen your results for your future the more you are able to align with your **intuition** to complete your deposit increase calculation. It will also help to build a solid foundation beneath you to move you to the next level in The Financial

Freedom System. This is vital because it is training you for all areas of your life, not just your finances.

With this stage you are developing a deeper relationship with your intuition, where it grows to be stronger than your ego. Using your intuition in this way enables you to stay strong and remain below the neck as your financial consciousness expands. Therefore, the transformation of this next break-through is that it profoundly develops your intuition with money and your finances.

Step 6:
Reach and Go Beyond Your Critical Mass

As you follow the system to reach and go beyond your Critical Mass, you will experience great improvements in your finances. However, benefits will occur across all areas of your life, not just in your finances. You may even be astounded by the multiple benefits you will gain in seemingly unrelated areas of your life.

Many clients report that after a few months of making deposits into their Foundation Account, they have more money available to them at the end of each month because they are unconsciously spending less. I see this occur again and again because as you build your foundation and your unconscious lets go of old limiting beliefs, you become more stable and relaxed. Therefore, you don't feel the need to spend as much on food, entertainment, or toys, so you spend less and retain more of your usual income.

A truly powerful impact of this process is that you become aware of your real needs versus your ego's inflated desires. This cuts mindless spending considerably, saving you more money!

Another benefit my clients have reported is that extra money comes into your life—money you never expected. Sometimes this comes in lump sum amounts, an increase in business income, or a pay raise. You become more attractive to money because of your newfound respect for it and for yourself.

Some additional benefits clients have experienced surprise even me!

- **Health**. One client reports that after he had been building his Foundation Account for a few months, he noticed the trash can in his family kitchen wasn't as full as usual each week. Before starting his Foundation Account, he had to empty it twice a week, but within a short space of time, he needed to empty it only once a week. He was amazed at how much less his family consumed when their stress was lower and how much happier they felt as a result. Plus, they all lost extra weight they had been carrying, so they felt healthier. Their food bill was also significantly lower, giving them more money at the end of the month. It was a win all around for this family.

- **Relationships**. Another client had been single for quite some time yet had been trying to find a partner to settle down with and marry, without luck. He said that once he began following my system, building his Foundation Account and feeling better about his finances, women seemed to be more attracted to him. This occurred even though he did not share with them his financial circumstances. Ultimately, he met and fell in love with a wonderful woman. They are now happily married and have started a family. This shift in his relationship situation came about as a very pleasant side benefit of his greater sense of love for himself and respect for his finances. As he became more secure, relaxed, and less stressed, the women around him felt safer and more at ease in his presence.

- **Family**. As your foundation grows and your relationships improve, you will likely also experience benefits in your family. One client explains that as he built his foundation, he felt happier and more relaxed. As this occurred, he found his usually busy mind gradually became more quiet and peaceful, resulting in better sleep and a general feeling of well-being. His improved state of mind allowed him to be more present and aware with his wife and children, so everyone experienced more joy and connection.

- **Business**. I often work with business owners, from those with small businesses to leaders of large organizations that employ hundreds of people. As these individuals build their foundations, they typically find their intuition improves, positively affecting their decision-making across all areas of their enterprises. With greater clarity, they become less stressed and more inclined to make wise choices for the future direction of their organizations, providing them with more enjoyment and fulfillment in their work.

- **Social Scene**. One of the most enjoyable benefits of building my foundation is in the area of my social life, especially after I achieved my 100 percent annual income goal. At this point and beyond, I was meeting and forming new friendships with like-minded people who also had a foundation. These individuals are from all walks of life and many different countries. They are relaxed and at peace with themselves and their lives, making it a pleasure to spend time with them. As I make my journey of inner transformation, I attract those on a similar trajectory, and this enriches my life even more.

- **Peace of Mind**. A peaceful mindset is a very real benefit of building your Foundation Account. The intangible nature of a calm mind is priceless. Recently, a client shared a wonderful example of how her newly created sense of inner peace helped her through a challenging time in her life. As a self-employed consultant and single mother, my client was accustomed to financially supporting herself and her son. However, she longed to experience a greater feeling of stability and security, so she was building her Foundation Account. Unfortunately, she became very ill, and she was unable to generate income or even look after her son for a number of weeks. She required temporary assistance from family and friends to care for her, her son, their family home, and their dog. Yet, she told me that while she was sick, not once did she worry about the drop in her income because she had peace of mind about her finances. She had a small amount of funds available in a regular bank account to draw on if she needed money in the event of an emergency. Plus, the fact that she had built her Foundation Account gave her a huge sense of security and peace. This inner peace enabled her to focus on regaining her health instead of stressing about her finances, and she bounced back in a short period of time. When she recommenced work, she commented that she had felt as if she could live on almost nothing, as her living expenses decreased and items she needed were gifted to her by friends and family or arrived in unexpected ways. Interestingly, the most important lesson she learned from the experience was that even though she had thought about using her savings if needed, she never considered touching the money in her Foundation Account. Her foundation was the key to her peace of mind, and the value of this was priceless in relation to her health and well-being.

THE TWELVE-MONTH TEST

As you experience greater feelings of peace, relaxation, and confidence with your finances, it is important to stay aware so you don't **think** you have reached your Critical Mass level prematurely. I call this **The Critical Mass Illusion**—you **think** you've made it because you are sensing financial freedom, but you're not there yet. Remember, Critical Mass is a transformed state of being; it is not just about reaching a preconceived figure in your Foundation Account. Yes, you will be feeling much better than you have felt before, but it doesn't mean you have actually reached **your** Critical Mass yet. When you can hold and maintain this energy in your body for twelve months, you have reached a new state of being, which is your authentic Critical Mass.

For example, clients sometimes become overly excited, thinking they have made it to their Critical Mass when the positive feelings and shift in their energy can actually be the result of outside influences. These influences can include positive changes in the weather, better energy in their family or community, or even dramatically improving economic conditions. Later, they become disappointed when their environment changes again and they lose these happy feelings.

To address this effect, once you think you have reached your Critical Mass level, see this as the starting point for what I call **The Twelve-Month Test**. This process will ensure you have truly achieved your Critical Mass, as well as keep you on track and moving toward your larger goal. I cannot stress strongly enough the importance of this because it is easy to become a little lazy and relaxed with your money and spending habits when your foundation is around your Critical Mass amount.

Continue to make your deposits for the next twelve months. Stay focused on the process during this time, and if the great feelings of inner peace and stability are consistent for the whole year, you know you have truly made it to your Critical Mass.

This is a testing time and a process of practicing discipline as you become stronger within. Rise above any negativity that tries to pull you back into unhealthy habits. When you feel you have achieved your goal, hang in there to cement the process and confirm your progress. Otherwise, you may allow the spirit of laziness to creep into your life. This may cause you to become so relaxed and ungrounded that you forget to make your regular weekly deposits or find yourself spending money unconsciously.

KEEP GOING

Completing The Twelve-Month Test after you think you have reached your Critical Mass level is a great milestone on your path to financial freedom. At this point, enthusiasm and confidence become normal, along with increased levels of energy and peace. There's no going back to your old ways now. You're transforming your unconscious, and new habits have taken root.

There might be temptation to stop following the system before you reach your Critical Mass, so stay focused. Once you break through to this point, your intuition and gut instinct will be stronger, and you'll be better inclined to take action based on what you feel is right for you.

Now, nobody and nothing can distract you from your mission or sell you on anything you don't need or want. Your spending will be more measured, and you now have much more money at the end of each month—more than enough for what you need. This is the point where you know you have reached your Critical Mass level.

MANAGING YOUR EXTRA MONEY

Now that you have arrived at your Critical Mass and continued past this level, it is essential to manage your **extra money**. This is money you have not spent in the course of your usual monthly living expenses, so it will feel like excess. You might be tempted to spend this money on trivial or unnecessary items. The ego might attempt to step back in and drive you to spend your extra money so it can regain power over you. As a result, you may sabotage your financial life at a stage where you have only just begun to truly experience the benefits of building your foundation.

Remember that you are also expanding your inner strength and defenses to protect against outside influences that might nudge you to give your power away. If you remain mindful and focused, you can maintain strength and centeredness in handling your money.

ESTABLISHING A SOLID SENSE OF SECURITY

I recommend that clients build a three-month supply of nonperishable goods in their homes to strengthen their foundation. This is done by focusing on one item at a time and building up the amount you have in storage until it reaches three months' supply. Once you reach this level with your first item, you move on to the second item, then the third, and so on. If you do this, you will also notice that the three-month supply of an item lasts longer than three months. Consequently, in the future you won't need to purchase as much to replenish your stock, and therefore you will have even more money left over each month.

The powerful benefits of this simple process was highlighted during the COVID-19 pandemic in 2020, when clients from all over the world reached out to thank me for advising them to build this part of their foundation. Instead of having to rush out to the supermarket before lockdowns, they had plenty of nonperishable foods, cleaning products, personal care items, pet supplies, and toilet paper on hand in their homes. They needed to buy only fresh produce to be fully prepared for a lockdown. This was a major source of peace and calm amid the fear and chaos of the pandemic.

Once you have completed building your three months' worth of supplies at home, I recommend that you work toward paying three months of your mortgage or rent in advance. An added benefit of this is that when you pay your financial responsibilities in advance, you energetically project a sense of security and prosperity. This alone brings lasting transformation to all areas of your life.

CRITICAL MASS GROWING WITH YOUR LIFE

As change is constant, there may be times when your perceived Critical Mass level shifts due to a change in circumstances. If your personal or family needs increase and suddenly you feel financial stress, continue building your Foundation Account until you again experience peace. I had a client who had reached his Critical Mass, and as a result, he experienced the financial ease and peace of mind that comes with this milestone. However, he became complacent and chose to stop making deposits during The Twelve-Month Test after he thought he had reached his Critical Mass level. Not long afterward, he learned a fascinating lesson on the power of maintaining deposits and growing the Foundation Account.

He was suddenly feeling stressed about his finances again. I asked him if anything had changed in his family or work environments, and he said, "No," but I was certain something had shifted to cause the stress. I recommended that he recommence building his foundation and assured him there was a reason for this change in his sense of inner peace and stability.

A short time later, he found out his wife was pregnant, so his family's foundation needs had completely changed. As he was the only one in the family who was building a Foundation Account, he was energetically responsible for the foundation for the entire family. He had intuitively felt the shift in energy and a requirement to build a larger foundation.

With this knowledge, he was inspired to complete the Critical Mass Twelve-Month Test and achieve the feeling of peace once more.

MY CRITICAL MASS EXPERIENCE

I clearly remember the experience of discovering my Critical Mass. It was an amazing feeling of relaxation in body and mind. Even when I had no money in my wallet, I felt free, I felt relaxed, and I experienced an inner sense of confidence.

Additionally, as I continued to build my Foundation Account, my regular transaction bank account was also growing, and excess funds were accumulating without effort. I now had a number of bank accounts that held as much money as my Critical Mass, and these were increasing in size each week. My business had grown substantially, and a steady stream of clients and work flowed toward me. I had money flowing effortlessly through my life, as well as having more than enough money on hand.

At the same time, I realized I didn't feel like spending money at all, because I had everything I needed. I wondered if something was wrong with me and thought, "What do I do now?"

I actually felt a little lost as the abundance and peace of mind I felt opened up all manner of new possibilities for me. I was now building up a treasure chest for the next opportunity as my options expanded. I asked myself questions about what I truly wanted in life, and this time, the answers arose from my soul. It was a strange sensation as I discovered that my soul had always been answering me, but I couldn't hear it before because of drama and stress in my life. I had reconnected with God and felt grounded and free. I now had the ability to ask my soul for guidance, and I received inspiration about my purpose and contribution.

I've seen many clients experience similar feelings. The freedom they felt allowed them to consider making life changes, such as going back to university, buying a new home, and doing what they want and love over what others expect of them.

STEP 6 CHECKLIST:
REACH AND GO BEYOND YOUR CRITICAL MASS

- **Continue to build** your Foundation Account until you reach and go beyond your Critical Mass.

- **Stay focused** with your deposits for an additional twelve months to solidify your Critical Mass strength.

- **Strengthen your position** by building three months' worth of supplies at home. Use your extra money each month to buy a three months' supply of one nonperishable item at a time. Then move on to the second item and so on.

- **Check your results** and acknowledge how much you've grown by following this system. Write down your results in your Financial Freedom Journal and, if you are happy to share your successes, contact us, as we would love to hear your stories. See details in the back of the book.

- **Experience the feeling** of how much more relaxed you are, even when you have no money in your pocket. Peace, stability, and emotional freedom come from the power of building a strong foundation for yourself. Enjoy!

COMMON QUESTIONS ANSWERED

Can I goal-set or predict my Critical Mass amount?

No. Before you reach your Critical Mass, there is no way of knowing or predicting what this amount will be for you. In fact, you will only discover this at the point at which you reach your personal Critical Mass. If you try to predict it, this is your ego taking control and distracting you from the transformation of your unconscious. However, once you reach your true Critical Mass, you will feel so different, so at ease and relaxed, that you will know you have reached this level in your Foundation Account.

Can I invest in other opportunities while building my Foundation Account?

Yes, but these are some recommendations to follow before you do so:

- Remain 100 percent committed to building a strong foundation, and continue following The Financial Freedom System steps before considering other opportunities.

- Use only your extra money to invest and never consider using funds from your Foundation Account.

- Consider whether or not the investment opportunity is a good fit within your current level of financial consciousness.

- To gain clarity on any opportunity, ask yourself these three questions before proceeding:

  * Have I paid myself first this week?

  * How do I feel intuitively when I reflect on the opportunity—weak or strong, excited or calm, in my ego or in my heart, looking for a fast result or focused on the long term?

  * How would I feel with 100 percent of my annual income in my Foundation Account?

What if I forget to make my weekly deposit?

Make your foundation deposit as soon as you remember.

One week, during my new Foundation Account process, the unthinkable happened: I forgot to make a deposit on a Monday and only realized this on Tuesday morning. I was surprised that I didn't feel any stress about missing the deposit. This lack of stress is probably because I had already achieved my Foundation Account goals ten years earlier. So, I placed my weekly deposit into my foundation jar.

Next, I had an ego reaction. My ego whispered fearful thoughts of my home being burgled and my Foundation Account jar being stolen. Due to my solid foundation, I was clear this fear was coming from ego. So, I wanted to explore how and why this deposit to my jar was negatively affecting me.

I did the two-minute breathing exercise to calm and center myself, and my intuition told me to count how much money I had accumulated in my Foundation Account jar. I had accumulated over $5,000 in my Foundation Account jar—my original Critical Mass level. Back then, my ego was triggered to take money out of the account to put into investments. Ultimately, these investments failed and I lost my money, so I was experiencing residual fear.

I wanted to break my ego's hold on me once and for all, so for the following week I did the breathing exercise every time I thought about my experience. As I did this, my ego-driven fear became weaker and weaker until it no longer had any power over me. This story reinforces the value of using intuition to address ego-driven fears.

After a few months, when I did my feeling check-in, why did the visualizations feel more energetically aligned?

When you started The Financial Freedom System, your annual income reflected the consciousness of where you were back then. As you build your Foundation Account, your unconscious also grows. Even if your current account balance is still low, your magnetic power to attract money increases along with your energetic stability and security. This *feels* positive and strong.

If you have any specific questions on Step 6 and would like them answered, write them down here or in your Financial Freedom Journal and join our next online event. See details in the back of this book.

FREEDOM BREAKTHROUGH: MASTERY AND RESPECT

It's time to celebrate. Once you have completed The Twelve-Month Test, you have reached the next breakthrough for the transformation of your relationship with money and finances.

Be sincere with this part of the process, as it will strengthen your results for your future. The more integrity you have with completing The Twelve-Month Test, the brighter and easier your future will be. This breakthrough is one of acknowledging the new level of **mastery and respect** you have built for yourself and your finances.

This is actually the most important breakthrough in your progress through The Financial Freedom System and will impact your life in a multitude of profound ways. The steps you took to achieve the earlier breakthroughs have brought you to the tipping point in your journey. You have undergone a transformation in your unconscious, just as coal under pressure transforms into a diamond. There is no going back to your old ways now.

At this stage, you live in integrity with your finances, your intuition is strong and clear, and you can consciously choose how best to manage and utilize your money. You have gained **respect** for your finances and become **the master of money**, and in return you are more attractive to money and opportunities in life. You have learned the key lessons of the system at this point and taken your life to a new level!

Step 7:
Enjoy Life

KEEP BUILDING YOUR FOUNDATION ACCOUNT UNTIL you reach the goal of having **100 percent of your original annual income, before taxes**, in your account. This is the figure you wrote down in the front of this book at the beginning of your journey.

This could take you five to ten years to achieve. I made many mistakes and corrections along the way, so my first 100 percent goal took me eight years. However, when I finally got there, I experienced a feeling like no other.

When you reach this goal, you too will notice how much better your life is and how much less stressed you feel about financial matters. Your visualizations have now become a reality.

Once you have your initial annual income in your Foundation Account, you have mastered your finances and your habits around spending and receiving. More positive energy and more income will move toward you. You will also develop a deep respect for the energy of money and for yourself.

Acknowledge yourself for reaching your goal and answer this question:

On what date did you achieve the goal of 100 percent of your annual income, before taxes, in your Foundation Account?

Date Achieved:

_____

Your answer will assist you with the next steps on your foundation journey.

MAINTAIN A PEAK LEVEL OF RESPECT

During this time, it is vital to maintain respect and humility in regard to your finances. I was given a significant lesson in maintaining respect for money at an early point during my financial freedom journey when I became arrogant and complacent.

I was in a supermarket one day in early 2002, and in the fresh produce section I saw a nickel on the floor. Instead of picking it up as a gift, my ego said I should leave it for someone who needed it. After all, I thought, it is only a small amount. That was my **first mistake**.

As I paid the cashier for my purchases and received my change, a nickel fell out of my hand and rolled down into a crack in the counter, never to be seen again. I didn't think much about it or ask the cashier for another nickel. Once again, I reasoned, it's only five cents. That was my **second mistake**.

As I arrived home, I pulled my keys out of my pocket and yet another nickel came tumbling out. I watched it roll down the driveway and fall into the street drain. That was my **third mistake**.

Now I thought, "Is this too much of a coincidence?"

An hour later, I met a client at a café. As I crossed the street, I opened my wallet and a five-dollar bill fell out and blew onto the middle of the road. The traffic was heavy, so I had to wait while watching it get blown around the street until it was safe for me to pick it up. At this point, **I admitted my mistakes** of being disrespectful with money and strongly asked for forgiveness. Never again would I disrespect any amount of money.

Since that time I do not overlook any money I spot on the ground. Each time I check in with my intuition to confirm whether to pick it up or not. As a result of this, I have had major breakthroughs in my business and personal life.

The first time this happened was in mid-2003 at the San Diego Airport as I was unloading my bags out of a friend's car. I noticed three pennies on the road. Sticking to my promise, I picked up the coins—without getting hit by traffic—and thanked God for the gift. I then flew to my destination and experienced the most successful two days of business since starting my career. I gave thanks to God for the successful trip, and my intuition reminded me of picking up the coins. I saw this as a confirmation.

A couple of years later, I was in a small village in Austria, getting out of a car to catch a train to go see another new client. As I picked up my bags, I spotted a two euro coin in the snow. I picked up the coin and thanked God for the gift. The following four days with my new client were amazing.

In 2007, as I was getting out of a taxi at the airport in Tokyo, I saw a bunch of coins on the ground. I dropped my bags and went to collect them. My friends, who were accompanying me, thought I was crazy, as we were running late for our flight. They saw them as only a few insignificant coins. I explained all the great results I'd had following similar acts, and they understood my actions.

I had even more breakthroughs in my career due to my renewed respect for money.

As you progress with the system and develop your relationship with your intuition, you will know if you are to pick up the money or not. Obey your intuition first!

100 PERCENT ACHIEVEMENT AT 100 PERCENT ANNUAL INCOME

Once you have reached this stage of development with your foundation, you will experience transformation as your reality. Having achieved such a huge long-term goal for yourself, you now have the confidence of knowing you can perform the same kind of transformation related to other major goals.

Many clients, by the time they reach this stage, find that they have so much extra money at the end of the month that they wonder what to do with it. I recommend keeping it in a savings account and then using this money to make life easier and more enjoyable for you and your family.

These are some examples of what clients have done with their extra money:

- Saved up for a deposit for their first home

- Bought a new car

- Purchased gold and silver bullion for the future

- Paid off their home mortgages

- Gone on the family holiday they always wanted

- Started an education fund for their children

- Paid off all bad debt

- Completed a renovation on the family home

- Started a business they always dreamed of

- Enjoyed a new hobby

- Employed a part-time cook and house cleaner

- Joined a gym and engaged a personal trainer

- Donated to favorite charities

What will you do with your extra money?

STEP 7 CHECKLIST: ENJOY LIFE

- **Reach 100 percent** by increasing your weekly deposits until you achieve the equivalent of your original annual income, before taxes, no matter how many years it takes!

- **Monitor money flow**. Each year monitor the changes in your income and expenses so you're consciously aware of the dynamics of how money flows through your life.

- **Acknowledge and celebrate** the achievement of the goal you set at the beginning of your lifetime transformational process.

- **Write in your journal**, describing your feelings and experiences of achieving this massive goal and the journey you took to get here. If you would like to share your journey with me and my team, please contact us—details are in the back of this book.

COMMON QUESTIONS ANSWERED

Can I transfer money from my Foundation Account into a higher-interest-bearing account?

Yes. At this stage in the system, you can. However, you must leave at least 35 percent of the total funds in your Foundation Account.

On my journey, I did this to protect myself and my Critical Mass amount from my ego. Once I rebuilt my Critical Mass—after I lost it due to some bad investment decisions—I deposited the $5,000 into a five-year fixed-term account. Because of the terms of this deposit, I couldn't touch it. This proved to be a good move. I could still feel the powerful effect of the Critical Mass as I continued to build my Foundation Account.

If you decide to move money from your Foundation Account, leave at least 35 percent of the funds in your Foundation Account as seed money to continue building your financial strength—unless your intuition guides you to leave more. You cannot take all of your money out of your Foundation Account. Honor your intuition instead of your ego.

What if I need to take some money from my Foundation Account to take care of unexpected problems that arise in my life?

Do everything in your power to avoid the urge to take money from your Foundation Account. Just imagine what would happen if you were to remove parts of the foundation of your home to patch up some holes in its walls above ground. Eventually your whole house would fall down. The same concept applies to your Foundation Account.

Taking money out of your Foundation Account to pay for problems in your life will cause weaknesses in your financial stability and dissipate the strength you have built up in your foundation. Even if life throws its worst at you and you are tempted to reach into your Foundation Account savings to rescue yourself, find the inspiration to come up with other solutions.

Of course, if you are completely stuck and the situation is desperate, then by all means use some of your Foundation Account money. Then continue your Foundation Account savings according to your normal weekly deposits to rebuild your foundation. I recommend that you revisit Step 3 to recalculate your position to confirm the correct weekly deposit amount for your recommencement point. This is important because you need to reassess where you are in relation to your current financial energy so you can continue forward with renewed confidence and commitment.

If you have any specific questions on Step 7 and would like them answered, write them down here or in your Financial Freedom Journal and join our next online event. See details in the back of this book.

Beyond Your Transformational Goal

AT THIS STAGE, YOU ARE PROBABLY EXPERIENCING THE feeling of having an overflow of abundance and freedom. You will also understand how this deeply affects your life and behaviors. The knowledge you have accumulated will enable you to set long-term goals and stick with them until you've achieved them. You will see how much you have grown physically, mentally, emotionally, and spiritually since the day you started this system.

Once you have reached 100 percent of your original annual income amount, you will have transformed your level of consciousness. This is an impactful part of the process. Now that you have achieved 100 percent of your original annual income goal and your tank is full, what is your next move?

As it has taken time to build your Foundation Account over a few years, your annual income has likely increased. You are now ready to move to the next level of your financial stability.

What is your new current annual income now that you have reached 100 percent of your starting annual income?

Please write your new annual income.

Amount:

_____

This becomes your new foundation goal.

Keep making deposits into your Foundation Account until you make up the difference between the two annual income amounts. This will happen much faster than it did with your previous amount. Once you reach the level of 100 percent of your new annual income in your Foundation Account, you have completed this process.

On what date did you reach 100 percent of your new annual income?

Date Achieved:

_____

With 100 percent of your new annual income in your Foundation Account, you have now transformed your financial consciousness for the future.

GOING BEYOND YOUR FOUNDATION ACCOUNT

In my experience, and with the clients who have followed my system, once you go beyond 100 percent of your new annual income, you have even more control over your spending and your finances. At this level, advertising and the media have much less power over you and your financial decisions.

When you do buy something, the best deal will effortlessly be presented to you, saving you time, money, and energy. You become very clear about what you want and what you have in your life. Your ego and its fears are much quieter, and now you experience life with greater clarity and peace.

It took me just over eight years to reach my original 100 percent annual income goal. As I was still experimenting with the system at the time, I decided to use some of that money to wipe out debts I had accumulated in building my business. I then promised myself I wouldn't take on anymore debt until I rebuilt my Foundation Account and would spend only money I had available.

I took enough money out of my Foundation Account to wipe out all of my bad debt and left the rest as the base to rebuild my Foundation Account to my then-current annual income. It took me four and a half years to build up to my new 100 percent annual income. I then used my Foundation Account amount as security to finance an office for my business. As a result of my new financial consciousness, I was able to pay off the whole mortgage for my office in seven years. All along, my 100 percent new annual income Foundation Account was still sitting in the bank.

By this stage in my journey, my life had transformed, as had my relationship with money. I was inwardly at peace and abundance flowed. The joy I experienced and the quality of new people who came into my life were way beyond what I ever encountered before I started along this path. I had developed a true abundance mentality.

COMMON QUESTIONS ANSWERED

How do I get rid of my debt?

Many books are written about how to get rid of your debt. The main point I want to emphasize here is that debt connects you to the stress of the creditor and drains you physically, mentally, and emotionally as you hold on to it. Do everything in your power to remove any debt, but not at the expense of building your Foundation Account.

Should I buy or rent a home?

This decision is always dependent on your ability to purchase a home in the current market conditions and is also linked to whether or not you have a down payment available to purchase or are saving up for a down payment. Regardless if you are buying or renting a home, you must always have your monthly repayment or rent at a level that is in integrity with your current financial situation and your unconscious ability to pay easily and effortlessly.

To take it to the next level of stability, have three months of rent or mortgage payments sitting in your regular bank account at all times.

What if I am starting my foundation later in life?

You are never too old to start building your foundation. The benefits you will receive by having more freedom and relaxation in your unconscious will positively affect your health, well-being, and enjoyment. The benefits you will receive along the journey with your weekly deposits—and in growing and protecting your foundation—will give you more strength and ability to enjoy life. After all, who wants to live their later years in a constant state of stress? It is never too late to start.

What if I am starting to build my foundation at twenty years of age?

That's fantastic and good for you! You will be way ahead of most of the population and experience all the benefits of financial freedom at a relatively young age. You will also reach your 100 percent annual income, before taxes, in your Foundation Account way before you are thirty years old.

I know families who started their children building their own foundations as young as eight years of age with pocket money and other creative part-time entrepreneurial activities.

If I had started my foundation when I was a kid cleaning windows in my neighborhood during school holidays, my life would have been completely different with the strength I would have achieved with a solid foundation. However, I took a different path and started my Foundation Account when I was thirty-two years old.

What can I do with the extra money I accumulate after Step 7?

I recommend leaving the original annual income amount in your Foundation Account or long-term deposit accounts, and keep building toward your new annual income. Any extra money you accumulate in your regular transaction accounts can be used in different ways. Some ideas include the following:

- Convert the difference into gold and silver bullion.

- Use it as a long-term investment in the stock market, if you understand and trust this area of investment.

- Place this amount into fixed-term deposits.

- Pay off the mortgage on your home, if you haven't done so already, thus removing debt, saving on interest payments, and increasing your financial equity.

- Use the amount to invest in real estate to create ongoing passive income.

If you have any specific questions on the "Beyond Your Transformational Goal" section and would like them answered, write them down here or in your Financial Freedom Journal and join our next online event. See details in the back of this book.

Take Responsibility for Your Life

I CAN'T PREDICT WHAT RESULTS AND BENEFITS YOU'LL personally experience by following The Financial Freedom System. Those will be your unique creation and will probably reach far beyond anything you imagined at the start of this process. What I can say for certain is that you'll be amazed by the sense of peace and freedom you will experience in many areas of your life.

It begins as you embrace your new financial freedom. You will be able to breathe deeply, filling your lungs with life-giving energy. Once you have created this new set of habits with money, you will experience a totally different reality in your life.

The real value of this system goes way beyond money. It's about living from a genuine experience of abundance that shows up in your state of well-being, relationships, and over-all approach to life.

When I started my business, I had dreams of being rich, but the truth turned out to be much bigger than that. I now have an amazing lifestyle filled with freedom, peace, and a lack of stress around finances.

THE BIG PICTURE OF AN ABUNDANT WORLD

It's hard for people to give to others when overwhelmed with financial stress. If all people of the world had the consciousness of security and abundance, there'd be a massive increase in contribution and a decrease in the amount of stress and illness in people's lives. The world would be a happier place for all.

We need to be able to hold the energy of abundance so that our bodies, minds, and consciousness have the chance to accept abundance as normal.

Imagine a world where this was the norm instead of the exception. How wonderful would this reality be?

The Seven Steps Simplified

CONGRATULATIONS ON PROGRESSING THIS FAR. To further reinforce the key concepts you have learned, the following is a quick review of the seven steps and how they work together to transform your life.

STOP DIGGING!

To start your journey to financial peace of mind and abundance, you must stop digging a financial hole. Stop trying to find get-rich-quick ways out of your financial situation and commit to building your foundation.

Your path to financial freedom lies in the transformational process of building your Foundation Account. Your Foundation Account is where you make weekly deposits, based upon the amount you can afford at the time. These are building solid, secure steps upward out of your financial hole on your journey from scarcity to abundance.

To stop digging your financial hole, change your habits with a strong intention by following the first four steps of The Financial Freedom System:

Step 1: Decide and Commit to The Financial Freedom System. Remember, deciding is making a choice above the neck; committing is taking action below the neck.

Step 2: Envision a Full Tank and create a clear vision of the transformation you'll experience by building your foundation. This gives you the all-important initial energy to take ongoing physical action toward achieving your goal.

Step 3: Calculate Reality since this amount needs to be real for you and not inflated by your ego or others' influences. Choose an amount for your weekly deposit that fits into your current budget and doesn't cause you financial stress.

Step 4: Deposit at the Bank and begin building your Foundation Account. Each time you make a deposit, you'll experience an increased level of energy and peace.

Once you have completed **Step 4** and made your initial deposit, you have reached your **first Freedom Breakthrough—integrity**.

Step 5: Grow and Protect by building your way out of your financial hole and growing toward your Critical Mass. Remember to stick to the system and maintain your weekly deposits and monthly increases. If you try to get out of the hole too fast by shortcutting the system, you will only find yourself digging another hole.

Once you have completed Step 5, you have reached your **next Freedom Breakthrough—intuition**.

The Critical Mass Illusion

Warning! Once you have built your foundation to a point where you have raised yourself partly out of your financial hole, you may think you have mastered money and reached your Critical Mass. Be careful! Your eyes are only seeing out of your financial hole, above ground. The Critical Mass Illusion is where the ego tries to trick you into thinking you have made it. In my experience, it takes at least another twelve months of weekly deposits to finally stabilize your foundation.

Step 6: Reach and Go Beyond Your Critical Mass means you have now built yourself out of your financial hole. During this time you have also built up your three months' supply of nonperishable goods at home and paid your mortgage or rent three months in advance.

By completing **The Twelve-Month Test**, you have now passed **your next Freedom Breakthrough—mastery and respect**.

Step 7: Enjoy Life as you grow your Foundation Account from your Critical Mass to 100 percent of your original annual income. Stay committed and disciplined to reach this transformational goal. Keep following the steps, making the weekly deposits, and growing your Foundation Account until you reach the important goal you established when you started The Financial Freedom System.

You have now completed all seven steps and are standing on solid financial ground.

Beyond Step 7: As it has taken time to build your Foundation Account over a few years, your annual income will have increased. Now you are ready to move to the next level of stability. Write down your new level of annual income, and keep making the deposits into your Foundation Account until you reach this new amount.

It's Not about the Money

A DEEPER BENEFIT

THROUGHOUT THIS BOOK I HAVE SHARED STORIES AND examples highlighting the many benefits of building a strong financial foundation. These benefits range from feelings of peace in your body and mind, financial freedom, improved relationships, greater health and joy in life, prosperity in business, gaining clarity of purpose, connecting with God and your intuition, and many more. However, perhaps the most profound impact is the spiritual transformation you will experience once you fully complete the seven steps outlined in my system.

When you have a solid foundation with money, your body and mind relax, and your ability to see clearly increases. Your gut instinct and intuition are also enhanced. Once you have physical, mental, and emotional relaxation, it is easier to open your heart, connect to your spiritual aspect, and come closer to God. This solid foundation gives you physical, mental, and emotional peace, inviting more energy to connect spiritually.

My transformational journey with my Foundation Account has brought me closer to God and my life's purpose, and it will do this for you too. Your relationship with God shifts from *needing God* to *wanting a relationship with God*. You want to connect with God's love consistently instead of pleading with God only when you need help.

This is a profoundly different state of energy from which to live because your connection with God is a blessing.

Are you ready to create this in your life?

Acknowledgments

I AM ETERNALLY GRATEFUL TO GOD AND MY INTUITION for helping me overcome my weaknesses around handling my finances. I still have a way to go to reach my big-picture goals, and I look forward to constant improvement along my path ahead.

Many friends, coaches, and family members have helped me on this journey. I look forward to personally thanking you and acknowledging your input in the realization of this book.

To all those who aspire to overcome perceived weaknesses with money and finances, I encourage you to persist with my transformational system so you can experience similar benefits and many more.

I look forward to hearing about your great success stories.

To your transformation,

Daniel White

About the Author

DANIEL (KIM) WHITE HAS BEEN CONSULTING SINCE 1994, having worked with clients in over forty countries. Recognized internationally for his unique intuitive gifts, he is a sought-after speaker and author. He works closely with his clients to help them overcome energetic blockages to abundance and financial freedom, empowering them to create better futures for themselves, their families, and their businesses.

Daniel's own struggles with finances inspired him to find a transformational solution that enabled him to build his financial freedom. He searched for answers to how financial habits and behaviors, as well as external energetic influences, can affect finances. The answers he discovered and the processes he developed during this search make his work and its results powerfully transformative. That's why he created *The Financial Freedom System,* and he teaches the seven-step process to clients around the world.

Originally from Perth, Western Australia, Daniel has a bachelor's degree in business administration from Northern Arizona University, where he attended on an athletic scholarship while training for selection on the 1992 Australian Olympic team. He continues to improve his ability to assist clients to transform their energy, environments, and relationships. He lives and works globally, still runs for fitness as well as pleasure, and enjoys great coffee and wonderful food with friends.

Contact
Daniel White

I would like to hear from you if you want to know more about any of the following:

- Connecting with me to learn more about my coaching services

- Accessing further ways for you to strengthen your foundation

- Joining my online Question-and-Answer or Group Transformation sessions

- Receiving regular newsletters and invitations to upcoming events

- Sharing your financial freedom stories and experiences

- Purchasing your copy of *The Financial Freedom Journal*

- Finding out about our other courses and trainings

Email Daniel or the team at daniel@danielwhitecoaching.com.

Visit his website at www.danielwhitecoaching.com.

Made in the USA
Monee, IL
14 June 2023